W0018207

Advance Praise

A short but effective book on Analytics which keeps business impact as key focus. A must read for every business leader and business manager to understand, evaluate and keep team working on analytics focused on needs of the business. The analysts would also benefit from this view. The vignettes in each chapter followed by approach to address the complication make for easy understanding.

Kalpana Margabandhu, Consultant and Director (Retired), India CIO Lab at IBM

I have known Arindam since the early nineties as part of the doctoral program. Arindam is one of the well-known thinkers and innovative voices in the world of analytics. Organizations that want to grow their analytical capability will benefit greatly from his keen insights on the development of world-class analytical capability and practice. Glad to know that Tanushri has joined him in imparting such useful professional advice.

Uday Kumar, Executive Director, Analytics and Optimization, Cox Communications, Atlanta

Having spent 30 years in Operations, Outsourcing, Business Development et al., I believe data has always been at the core of it all. Seeing patterns, connecting to insights to drive actions or decisions is the only way to make data work for you intelligently. Companies have so much data available which they do not know how to make best use of. An integrated solution is all about weaving Analytics into process and technology to drive superior results across all aspects of an Organizational life-cycle, be it in recruiting, training, running daily operations, improving performance, driving productivity, quality or profitability. Its applicability continues to grow, be it Healthcare, Location based services, Retail or Manufacturing. I believe the book provides a strong foundation for building effective Analytics capability in organizations irrespective of the business context – something all decision makers may want to review.

Anju Talwar, CEO, The Skills Academy,
(SVP Genpact, ex-American Express)

This book is meant for business managers/leader, who would like to manage Analytics processes and projects effectively for better business decision making. With a business use case perspective, it goes over the problem solving approach, stages of a typical analytics initiative and how to monitor productivity of analytical output.

Priya Jha Dang, Knowledge Business Director,
Strategy PA, Boston Consulting Group

One of the best primers on the 'complex' subject of business analytics targeted at practising managers! A first of its kind!

The authors provide a concise, highly accessible yet non-technical explanation of the concepts that underlie the various tools and techniques. The innovative use of the vignettes at the beginning of each chapter as well as the caselets interspersed in between helps one relate to the specific situations and gain a profound understanding of potential applications in one's own context. Here's the best part: Although the authors' presentation is comprehensive, they explain everything without the use of advance Math.

Highly recommended for any manager interested in this subject; it really delivers.

Sunil Raj, Group Manager (Jewellery),
Titan Company Ltd

Weaving Analytics for Decision Making is a book for business managers/leaders who are not technically trained but are looking at managing Analytics processes and projects effectively for improved business decision making. This book can also be taken up as 'Analytics for business managers' as it gives 360 degree view of analytics than just focusing on various types of analytical methods.

Poonam Bareja, Head Business Technology and Analytics, Marico Limited, Mumbai

Weaving Analytics for Effective Decision Making

Weaving Analytics for Effective Decision Making

Arindam Banerjee
Tanushri Banerjee

Los Angeles I London I New Delhi
Singapore I Washington DC I Melbourne

First published in 2017 by

SAGE Publications India Pvt Ltd
B1/I-1 Mohan Cooperative Industrial Area
Mathura Road, New Delhi 110 044, India
www.sagepub.in

SAGE Publications Inc
2455 Teller Road
Thousand Oaks, California 91320, USA

SAGE Publications Ltd
1 Oliver's Yard, 55 City Road
London EC1Y 1SP, United Kingdom

SAGE Publications Asia-Pacific Pte Ltd
3 Church Street
#10-04 Samsung Hub
Singapore 049483

Published by Vivek Mehra for SAGE Publications India Pvt Ltd, typeset in 11/14 pt Helvetica by, JMV Design Solutions, Chandigarh 31D and printed at Chaman Enterprises, New Delhi.

Library of Congress Cataloging-in-Publication Data

Names: Banerjee, Arindam, 1965- author. I Banerjee, Tanushri, author.
Title: Weaving analytics for effective decision making / Arindam Banerjee, Professor of Marketing, IIM Ahmedabad, Tanushri Banerjee, Associate Professor, Pandit Deendayal Petroleum University, Gandhinagar.
Description: Thousand Oaks : SAGE Publications India Pvt Ltd, [2017]
Identifiers: LCCN 2017019960 (print) I LCCN 2017032653 (ebook) I ISBN 9789386446787 (e-book) I ISBN 9789386446763 (pb)
Subjects: LCSH: Industrial management—Decision making—Data processing. I Business—Decision making—Data processing.
Classification: LCC HD30.2 (ebook) I LCC HD30.2 .B3576 2017 (print) I DDC 658.4/032—dc23
LC record available at https://lccn.loc.gov/2017019960

ISBN: 978-93-864-4676-3 (PB)

SAGE Team: Manisha Mathews, Apoorva Mathur and Ritu Chopra

Dedicated to our Parents

Thank you for choosing a SAGE product!
If you have any comment, observation or feedback,
I would like to personally hear from you.
Please write to me at **contactceo@sagepub.in**

Vivek Mehra, Managing Director and CEO, SAGE India.

Bulk Sales

SAGE India offers special discounts
for purchase of books in bulk.
We also make available special imprints
and excerpts from our books on demand.

For orders and enquiries, write to us at

Marketing Department
SAGE Publications India Pvt Ltd
B1/I-1, Mohan Cooperative Industrial Area
Mathura Road, Post Bag 7
New Delhi 110044, India

E-mail us at **marketing@sagepub.in**

Get to know more about SAGE

Be invited to SAGE events, get on our mailing list.
Write today to **marketing@sagepub.in**

This book is also available as an e-book.

Contents

Foreword

With more than three decades of experience in academia along with working for large corporations to develop data-driven corporate decisions, Dr Arindam and Dr Tanushri have brought together the unique combination of academics and practice in this guide book that will help corporate decision makers navigate the complex and ever-evolving maze of analytics. While much of what is today called as data science perhaps germinated in academia, the last decade has seen an explosion of its use in business decision making. Equally, there has been a significant growth of 'techniques' and technology on how to access and analyse data, pushing businesses to commit scarce corporate resources, both money and people, in the pursuit of better decisions.

Today's business leaders have multiple approaches and sources to provide them with the insights needed to improve decision making; however, there is a high probability of getting trapped into the 'how' or the technique of developing the insights than 'what' or prioritizing the insight that drives the right decision. This guide book clarifies and provides a good control tower view of business decision making using data-driven insights.

By arranging the chapters that replicate typical decision processes in organizations, the authors have used many live examples to illustrate and bring to life the practical aspects and issues that need to be addressed to integrate data-led decision-making process along with 'gut feel' in the board room. The authors have equally focused on one time projects versus building long-term skill and sustaining capability in the organization to help harness a robust decision-making process.

Finally, this guide book is for decision makers looking to build a sustainable capability in data science to complement their decision-making process. It will also be very helpful for those who have already invested in analytical ability to revisit and reprioritize their future investments to help make key decisions that drive business.

I invite the reader (be it a business leader or an analyst) to actively refer to this book while they grapple with their challenges of data-driven business problem-solving initiatives. On one hand, while it serves as a good complement to manuscripts that essentially focus on analytic techniques, it also helps buttress the efficacy of analytic initiatives with its mission to be primarily focused on the business objectives.

Badri Veeraghanta,
Partner,
A.T. Kearney, Singapore

Preface

At the outset, let us state that this book is written for decision makers who would like to invest in Analytics as a support for their work. We are not going to explain the virtues of Analytics. It is assumed that the reader is already convinced about its worth.

The book will also help data scientists and other analysts who work with large databases, but would like to reorient their work to better serve business decision-making activities. This is an important dimension of Analytics that does not get much prominence and therefore is the primary motivation for us to write this book. Based on our own experience, let us also try to describe why this theme is important in the current context in India.

Our 'brush' with Analytics spans over 25 years now. It includes initially working on model building using large-scaled data in the retail space in the United States in the early nineties using SAS and other contemporary software tools. At that time, no one really called this function as Analytics. The nomenclature came much later.

While we thrived on the opportunities in information sciences and analytics that came our way, little did we realize that the skills that we learnt back then to solve pertinent problems for business would someday become titled as the 'sexiest profession' (quote from *Harvard Business Review*, October 2012 issue). At least, when some of us went through the grind many years ago, it did not look so exciting. It was more like an essential component of managerial decision making. What was never envisaged, back then, was that it had the potential to become the next hot spot in career options for a youngster (as it is currently pitched). In fact, at the turn of the century, India as a market was still not ready for this type of expertise. We have personally faced situations where industry leaders have frowned upon this function as something not too critical for Indian business operations. What then created this 'brouhaha' in the corporate world that led to a dramatic change in the fortune of professionals involved in this trade?

For one, at the turn of the century, enterprises in the developed economies started selectively shifting processes to the developing world to overcome the disadvantage of operating in a high labour cost environment. As a result, technologically sophisticated processes moved to geographies which provided abundant 'techno-trained' and cheap resources and analytics was one such process.

Influx of new processes which were technologically advanced obviously led to heightened interest in the domestic corporate landscape regarding this new function. At the same time, entry of analytically skilled labour and talent from across borders also led to an overall escalation in curiosity about its advantage to businesses. From the middle of the first decade of the 21st century, Analytics took rapid steps to tease the minds of decision makers in India. Increased competition in the domestic market additionally helped spurt the interest in Analytics.

Interestingly, Analytics has taken a skewed turn in India, given that parts of the function were selectively imported keeping the focus on the technological aspect of the domain. Data science was the centrepiece, although the original business model for organizations in the Western world did not make these sub-parts of Analytics separable entities. In India however, Analytics processes quickly focused on the technical elements of analytics, aka, modelling and predictive power.

This trend should naturally perplex business decision makers who manage businesses and do not necessarily want to manage specialized processes, without seeing a connection between the process output and its impact on business. A professional acquaintance who has been managing marketing intelligence function for large consumer organizations in the United States for years, quipped:

> It is the political divide between the East Coast-based consumer products companies and the West Coast-based technology companies. Analytics, in the East Coast (companies) is more evolutionary and centred around business problem-solving using data. However, the technology companies on the West Coast have focused more on the technology platforms and data science and touted them as the drivers of business Analytics.

India may have been exposed more to the ideas emanating from the technology-based companies in recent times. While this may be sweeping generalization, it is still worth a thought.

The focus of this book, as stated earlier, is squarely on the dilemma faced by the decision maker of an Indian business. It stays clear of the objective of promoting data science; instead it provides guidance on how business leaders should use analytics as a catalyst to solve business problems. The emphasis is on solving business problems and not on the technology.

Hopefully, it will provide guidance to decision makers on how to evaluate investments in analytics project (or process) for their organization and what may be an effective way to adopt such expertise over time, with an unflinching focus on business impact. At the same time, it will complement the role of data science.

This unique positioning of the book should add value to the learning on the practice of Analytics and hopefully be a useful reference to both decision makers as well as to the analysts. For the latter, it should provide helpful tips to fine tune their analytical output to make them more user friendly for businesses.

The book is organized into two distinct parts. Part I (Introduction to Chapter 5) provides an approach to decision makers on how to build an effective analytics process. It also provides an exposure to the various kinds of Analytical methods and infrastructure that are used in practice.

The Introduction specifically ignites the dilemma of many business leaders about how they should initiate and direct their organization's analytic capabilities. Chapters 1–4 provide some guidance on how to resolve such problems.

Chapter 5 provides a view on how to evaluate infrastructure to support the analytics process. While the theme of the book remains focussed on providing business leaders with an approach to making their analyses more meaningful, no one can shy away from the challenge of upscaling this initiative, once the concept is proven. We discuss the challenge of scaling up analytics through building appropriate infrastructure and its impact on the organization culture in this chapter.

Part II is a commentary of the analytics landscape, as is today, with a focus on India. Chapter 6 provides insights into the real challenges that organizations are facing in ramping up productivity. This is based on our research study, the perspectives of various analytics managers and also our findings from in-depth studies of a few organizations on the state of development of analytics practices in India. It provides insights on the evolution, potential challenges and opportunities that Indian organizations face as they develop their internal analytics prowess for sustaining competitive advantage.

We hope you will find the book useful.

Acknowledgements

Both of us would like to acknowledge the immense contribution made by our respective employers (IIM Ahmedabad and Pandit Deendayal Petroleum University) in providing a very productive academic environment for us, to (a) interact with enthusiastic students and business professionals, (b) research on topical issues faced in the Analytics domain and (c) facilitate documenting our ideas and thoughts on developing new approaches to the practice. It would not have been possible to get this manuscript ready without the support of this healthy collegial environment.

We would also like to thank our academic colleagues for their constant support and feedback in numerous internal forums which have sharpened our thinking around the content of this book. To the participants of various executive programs on Analytics that we have conducted, a special thank you for the diverse ideas that sprang up from them during the course of some very spirited discussions.

Finally, we appreciate the encouragement provided by our parents and siblings. Without their support and motivation over time, this project could not have been accomplished. The enthusiasm and affection of our children, Antara and Dhruv, led us to stay focused and devote time to conceive this manuscript.

This book is partially supported by a grant from the Research and Publication Office of IIM Ahmedabad.

Arindam Banerjee
Tanushri Banerjee

PART 1

An Approach to Build Analytics
Capability to Solve Business Problems

Introduction

The Practice of Analytics and the Associated 'Conundrum'

*L*et us consider a retail environment where a customer *is evaluating a possible purchase (see Figure I.1). The manager of the retail store would be interested in knowing whether she would pick-up the product that she is reviewing. More importantly, the store manager will be interested in knowing the process that the consumer applies to take a decision and what might be the drivers of the process. For instance, the manager would like to know, (a) who is the customer, (b) what is she thinking about the product, (c) what are the qualities of the product she is evaluating and (d) what is the final decision taken by her (to buy/or not to buy). You will appreciate that this information will be useful for the manager to evaluate the purchase situation and associate the behaviour of the customer to the various contextual and customer parameters. It is presumed that this exercise will yield insights about customers and retail parameters that influence sales, which the manager can smartly use to develop better selling strategies in the retail store.*

The 'Art of Analytics' is about creatively crafting insights from data available in a business environment for effective

Figure I.1   The Constituents of an Analytics Process

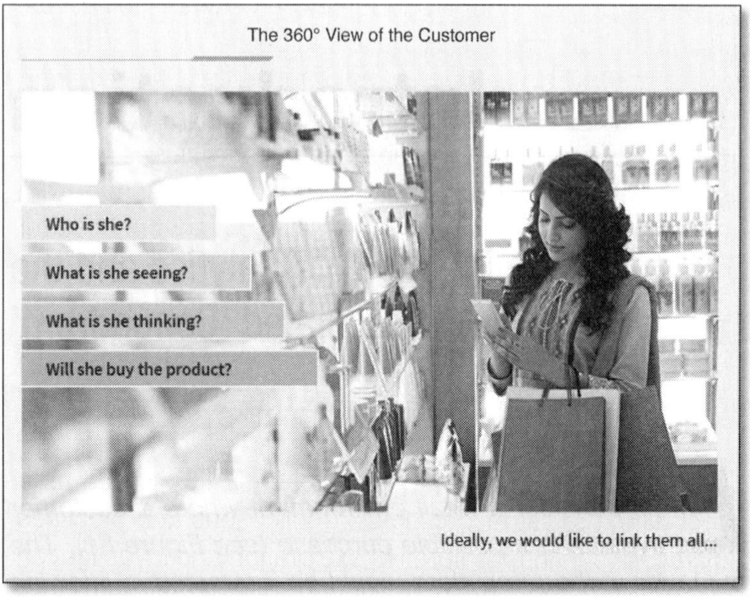

The 360° View of the Customer

Who is she?

What is she seeing?

What is she thinking?

Will she buy the product?

Ideally, we would like to link them all...

use in developing future managerial interventions of the type described previously. The challenge, many times, is about implementing such objectives successfully, clawing through the myriad issues of 'misaligned' data, incomplete information, incomprehensible analysis and uninterpretable output.

Hopefully, by the end of this book, there will be some succour from such seemingly insurmountable challenges.

Introduction

Analytics is usually defined in practice as any fact-based deliberation which leads to insights (diagnostics) and possible implications for planning future action (as we described in the vignette above). It could range from routine tracking and monitoring of business performance, 'nice-to-know' validation facts regarding the business domain, to more directed diagnosis of 'root cause' of business problems as well as strategic prediction about future business initiatives. The commonality across all these exercises is that it is driven significantly by facts ('rational' by nature) obtained as a part of business and market data collection initiatives by firms. The need for factual evidence-based inference as an input to the business decision process has been in vogue from early times of management history. With the advent of better information-gathering process and processing tools, more structured insight building from information is currently the standard expectation in the industry.

The Analytics Domain as it is Today

'Business Analytics' is often times defined in practice as a 'set of all the skills, technologies, applications and practices required for continuous iterative exploration and investigation of past business performance to gain insight and drive business planning'.[1] This process can, depending upon its outcomes, be descriptive, diagnostic, predictive and prescriptive in nature.[2]
Some illustrative analytical approaches are:

1. Describing a phenomenon through different measures that could capture its relevant dimensions is Descriptive Analytics. The purpose is to simply unravel 'what happened' or alerting on what is happening.

    It could be a dashboard-like application when an organization routinely generates various metrics using

---

[1] Michael J. Beller and Alan Barnett, 'Next Generation Business Analytics,' 2009. Retrieved from https://www.slideshare.net/LightshipPartners/next-generation-business-analytics-presentation, accessed on 21 January 2017.

[2] Gartner Report 'Forecast: Enterprise Software Markets, Worldwide, 2011–2016, 4Q12 Update,' 2012. Retrieved from https://www.gartner.com/doc/2272115/forecast-enterprise-software-markets-worldwide, accessed on 23 December 2016.

data to monitor a process or multiple processes across time. Any decision support system falls into this category. What is important even in such routine applications is to interpret these numbers and meaningfully connect it with the understanding of the underlying process or processes relevant to decision making. For such analytics applications, one needs to cultivate the skill of reading relevant facts from figures, of connecting it with the relevant decision-making process and finally of taking a data-driven decision from the business point of view. Usually such analytics is used repetitively and routinely in an organization for day-to-day operations.

2. To evaluate 'why' something happened is Diagnostic Analytics. It needs exploratory data analysis of the existing data or additional data, if required, to be collected using tools such as visualization techniques in order to discover the root causes of a problem.

These analyses are investigative in nature. They could be either exploratory or confirmatory. For such applications, organizations usually hire consultants or business 'sleuths'. Given a business objective, the tasks of the sleuths could be to frame relevant research questions, collect appropriate data and then analyse it intelligently to answer it and finally to connect the findings with the business objective. Often, during the data collection or analysis stage, some interesting patterns could emerge that were not known before and are considered to be surprising discoveries. For this kind of applications, one needs to be smart in posing relevant questions, in answering it intelligently with appropriate data, possessing skills of exploring data with the mind of a sleuth and finally connecting the findings with the business objective. Such applications are useful in under-standing the business environment, the customers, the risks associated with a new product, etc., generally in making strategic decisions. Such analytics are used many times for forward looking decision making. We could categorize these attempts as 'Diagnostic' or, in some instances where there are direct implications on the future, as 'Predictive' analytics.

3. To seek options for future business imperatives, Predictive Analytics is used. Predictive Analytics is to predict potential future outcomes and explain drivers of the observed phenomena using statistical or data mining techniques. It may be like predicting the sales of a product in the next month or the behaviour of a target segment of the customers.

4. Prescriptive Analytics goes to the extent of suggesting 'what courses of action may be taken' for the future to optimize business processes to achieve business objectives. In other words, it associates decision alternatives with the prediction of outcomes. For Prescriptive Analytics, Decision Analysis is used which includes tools such as optimization and simulation.

Unfortunately, there are very few examples of good 'Prescriptive' Analytics in the real world. A good reason for the shortfall is that most databases are constrained on the number of dimensions that they capture. Hence, the analysis from such data provides, at best, partial insights to a complex business problem. Most Prescriptive Analytics exercises are therefore half-baked and need to be used with caution. Nevertheless, business analysts have devised 'scenario builders' based on statistical analysis of market response data,[3] which provide elasticity measures (impacts) of different

---

[3] An example of market response data would be sales data of a business organization.

managerially controlled parameters.[4] Using them, they have devised 'what if' simulators that help provides insights about what may be the plausible options that the business ought to implement in order to maintain or strengthen its position in the market.

5. There is another 'category' of analytics, which appears to be more of a buzz word in today's analytics parlance, which is 'Big Data Analytics'. Today's companies process more than 60 terabytes of data annually which is 1000 times more than what they used to do a decade ago. Also, huge amount of data are generated by individuals spread across different geographic regions in different formats like texts, videos, tweets, blogs, etc. More importantly in 1986, only 6 percent of the world's data were in digital format compared to 90 percent in today's world. So the real concern is to make use of this huge volume of data to derive meaningful insights and drive fact-based decisions for business success. In Big Data world, filtering the signal out of noise is the key. Mostly, the analytics is exploratory (descriptive) in nature. By making use of exploratory statistical methods (data mining tools), the sole objective is to discover meaningful patterns or unknown correlations that could be used for making business decisions. There have been growing concerns regarding the reliability (veracity) and the usefulness (value) of these massive data forms and therefore a nagging question remains of the returns to the investment of processing such data forms.

In a nutshell, business analytics supposedly spans the past, present and future to give us more knowledge, better

---

[4] An example of managerially controlled parameters is marketing mix parameters such as product features, price, advertising, etc.

information and concrete insights. It tends to get more complex and valuable as it moves from descriptive to prescriptive applications.

The Decision Maker's Dilemma

In the current scenario, the corporate world seems very positive about the virtues of analytics. Many conversations in the world of analytics are dominated by the successes made by many digitally connected organizations (examples quoted often times are of Google and Amazon) and their ability to work with data to get better at their business forays. Opinion makers in this field are many, and they all believe in the future of business driven by data and insights from data using Analytics processes.

However, the business leader (and the reader) in an average organization, not necessarily operating in the digital space, is bound to remain puzzled by this professed growth story. Given that large-scale digital data is confined mainly to organizations in the e-commerce industry, the question that begs an answer is: How should leaders in a typical organization evaluate the analytics growth potential for their firm? This book will try to provide some leads towards helping business leaders look at an appropriate way to manage their investments in this new emerging capability.

'New' and 'Emerging' are somewhat incongruous to the idea of Analytics. Analysis has been a perpetual input into business decision making. However, in recent times with the advent of analytics as a new form of analysis and linked often times to a much significant role of the computation algorithms, many decision makers in organizations seem somewhat befuddled about appropriately positioning this new capability in the overall realm of decision making. Often times, questions are raised about whether this capability would substitute for traditional ways of making decisions, and how would that happen given that machine-learning algorithms may not match up with the 'quality of decision making' (comprehensive evaluation) that collective human wisdom may derive, in spite of the former's 'power of consistency'. These issues have fuelled extensive discussion in the practice world without enabling clear answers.

In our practice experience, the best description of productive Analytical capability in an organization was offered by a 30-year veteran in a financial services organization. When asked how he would describe the role of an analytics professional in an organization, he quipped, 'Her job is to tell meaningful business stories which are useful inputs into decision making...except that the stories are always backed by data'. Hence, going by this assertion, we believe that in the world of productive analytics, organizations strive to back their decisions with evidences from business data (as far as possible). When data is not available, heuristics and 'gut feel' are used to fill up the gaps. However, the 'assumptions' based on heuristics and gut feel need to be adequately vetted (stress tested) to ensure that they are to a reasonable degree appropriate— we note that this process is also called 'triangulation'.

Is there a role of computers and algorithms in this notion of analytics? Sure there is. Except that the role is more in terms of infrastructural support to process large-scale data rather than a central role that substitutes for 'insight development' and defining 'so what' (implications), the latter being something best left to the evolved analyst.

The tacit capability of the analyst in converting 'evidence' into 'implication' remains as important today in the world of analytics as it was earlier. However, what has changed is the computational tools and implements used by the analyst today to extract evidences, and the decision makers must carefully evaluate this transition for their organizations to invest wisely in appropriate capabilities.

Required Analytic Skills

The conditions for Analysis to flourish in organizations require different kinds of skills to be blended together. The skill set required to leverage its advantages is a concoction of data management skills, statistical/data processing prowess and business acumen. The Analytics resource with the 'right' mix (Figure I.2) is in high demand, and not surprisingly, is available in short supply. Most organizations, in reality, have evolved their analytic processes around a mix of resources that have varying strengths in more than one of the three key strengths.

1. DATA INVENTORY MANAGEMENT

Scientific enquiry requires regulated data formats that provide easy evaluation of (in)consistency in the patterns among the data, a requirement for good quality analytics. The new age analysts needs to be conversant with the format of the organizational data inventory and be able to 'pull' the right data bytes from storage to be able to offer the 'right' information. Increasingly, the familiarity with unstructured data is also known to be important.

2. PROCESSING CAPABILITIES

This is something that was always an integral part of business analysis. However, with the advent of large-scale databases, knowledge of sophisticated data-processing engines (software- and model-building capabilities) is fast becoming a necessity, in order to mine insights from big pools of data. This is one capability that organizations find easiest to acquire, given the large number of institutions that impart training. The market today has been a proliferation of this skill. It is also easy for the analysts to make themselves marketable, since this a 'visible' and useful (though not sufficient) capability for analytics to fructify.

Figure I.2   The Skill Requirement of an Analytics Process

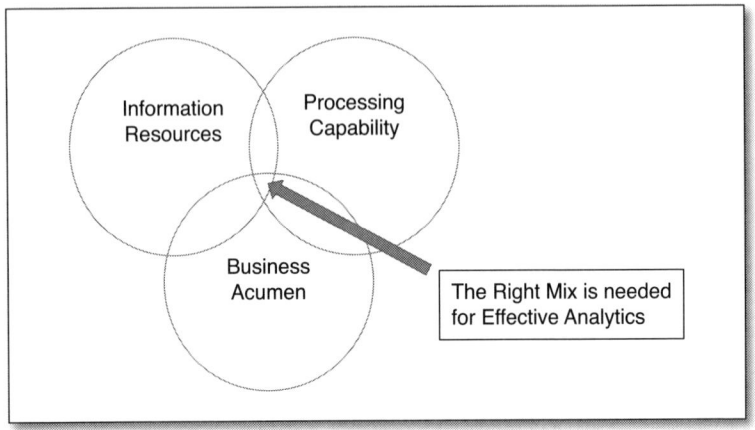

Source: Banerjee, Bandyopadhyay and Acharya (2013).[5]

3. BUSINESS ACUMEN

No one can ignore the importance of converting data to meaningful insights and implications. This capability, generically termed as Business Acumen, is actually a mix of business conceptual knowledge along with contextual familiarity. Without this skill set, data analytics capability is at best a processing department within the organization that churns 'insipid' reports.

Business leaders trying to reap the benefits of data insights need to encourage executives with high business acumen to excel in developing data-driven insight development skills. The latter need to be comfortable reading data insights and developing the knack of connecting them with their business relevance.

Not the easiest capability to be developed. Usually, resources having specialized processing skills and having

---

[5] Banerjee, Arindam, Bandyopadhyay, Tathagata & Acharya, Prachi (2013). 'Data Analytics: Hyped Up Aspirations or True Potential?' *Vikalpa*, 38(4), 1–11.

the urge and capability to participate into actively business decision making have the right mix of skills to drive this activity. However, unlike processing skills which can be imparted through training programs, today's analytics skill is a strange mixture of data literacy and creative business acumen that develops with exposure to various business problem contexts.

Many organizations, especially in developed markets, which are in an evolved state of adoption of analytics, have embedded skills where policy development groups have additional expertise in data processing and management. Usually, the career graph of employees in such analytically savvy organizations requires them to transition from data-processing responsibilities to policy making with opportunities to move back and forth as required. Such organizations usually have blended skills in their employees over time and do not usually depend on specialists to manage analytical tasks. However, as mentioned earlier, this kind of evolution takes time and a proper organizational culture has to set in to make it happen successfully.

Challenge of Setting Analytics Culture in Organizations

Analytics-driven culture takes time to build and gain acceptance, and a typical analytics rich organization has right data management practises, right set of professionals, right mindset and right amount of patience to see the fructification of analytics initiatives over time. In such organizations, analytics are introduced with a strong belief, and spearheaded from induction to practise to adoption, by the top management, with conviction.

Besides the general teething problems of an evolving practice, there are some unique complications in this domain, such as the supposed incompatibility between the skill sets required for, (a) managing information, (b) processing the information especially if it is in large scale and, (c) developing implications out of the processing results which connect to a resolution of the business problem using domain knowledge. Historically, these three disciplines have largely stayed distant from each other and hence the need for their synergetic association was never directly required. Research and Analytics based decision making processes have forced these three hitherto unassociated skills to integrate. So far, no skill development programs for management, to our knowledge, have focused on the integration of these three skills at a large scale as it is required today.

This is perhaps the reason why analytics has different connotations in various settings. In organizations heavily invested in data resources, data-processing and business modelling capabilities such as digital marketing companies, analytics is synonymous to statistical modelling/text mining. For instance, past purchase data of customers are used to conduct profiling and purchase basket analysis at customer level and, 'offtake sensitivity to marketing ploys' analysis at product level, to ascertain optimal marketing campaigns both at the individual customer level and at the market level for better business performance.

In organizations used to large-scale MIS report generation, the role of analytics is limited to Business Intelligence Processes. Many process industries fall under this category. Process control architecture generates streaming data on process parameters that are collated in the form of continuous MIS to monitor the overall operations. Oil refineries and chemical industries are prime examples of such large-scale application of MIS in operational monitoring.

Organizations with disparate set of relatively small databases pertaining to parts of the business operations have a hard time defining an uber Analytics capability, since their processes are not compatible with large end data processing. Many traditional marketing organizations of consumer goods have a repository of market research and internal data in multiple formats which lend themselves to piecemeal analyses. For instance, there may be a large data base of consumer perceptions about brands using survey-based tracking methods. Separately, a household panel is used to track consumer purchase data. Many of these initiatives come under the function of market research. Simultaneously, the organization may be tracking shipment data on outbound goods in their enterprise resource planning (ERP) system. Accounting systems provide information about revenue and profitability of different business units.

These different systems provide information useful to track the performance of the business. However, there is no mechanism that is able to reconcile metrics from different systems to provide an overall view of the business performance. The reconciliation still remains largely a matter of perception of the analyst.

Outsourcing Analytics: Another Challenge to Creating Productive Analytic Culture

In the past 15 years, outsourcing of processes (particularly analytics) to distant geographic locales which have both cost advantage as well as specialized data-processing capabilities have led to the evolution of the current stream of Analytics dominated by statistical and computational prowess. While its virtues are being debated, this separation of a few Analytic capabilities from others mentioned earlier have spurred more imbalances in the capability in many organizations and taken them away from the blended resources that have been talked about in an earlier section.

The prime mover for outsourcing Analytics processes to low-cost environs has been cost management. However, imbalances have been caused because business acumen is critical to boost up value addition in the analytics process. Low-cost environs which provide offshore services are associated with market conditions which are not compatible with the developed markets for whom the analytical services are rendered. The ability for resources in the offshore environ to appreciate the nuances of domain knowledge of the user (developed) markets is limited, leading to the possibility of suboptimal output. In general, technology in the form of processing capability (surfeit in its availability in low cost environ) acts as a poor substitute for business acumen to drive value addition.

Inevitably, the ideal solution to these challenges lies in the cross pollination of skills both within and across environs to improve the competency set. Migration of experts from the domain, development of offshore environs and better work/information flows across work sites/personnel with differential skill sets can help alleviate the challenges over time.[6]

This trend towards specialization has inevitably led to the development of analytics as a process rather than a philosophy of organizations to take rigorously deliberated decisions.

Also observed are the proliferation of specialist firms providing data processing help (stats modelling) without commensurate knowledge of business context to provide quality business advisory services.

Usually, these specialist firms have evolved into the Analytics domain using their traditional strengths in the Knowledge industry. For instance, the traditional information

---

[6] Banerjee, Arindam and A. Williams, Scott (2009). International Service Outsourcing: Using Offshore Analytics to Identify Determinants of Value-added Outsourcing. *Strategic Outsourcing: An International Journal*, 2(1), 68–79.

management firms (for example, Wipro, Infosys) have veered towards automation and reporting processes (Descriptive Analytics). Whereas, the algorithm building firms (for example, SAS, IBM), would be better positioned as modelling and optimization specialists (Predictive and Diagnostic Analytics). Traditional Business advisory firms (for example, McKinsey, BCG, Monitor) tend to rely on their domain skills to provide prescriptions for business problems while depending on more specialized data-processing partners to provide them with the analysis. The jury is still out regarding the usefulness of such specialized and piecemeal measures.

Such proliferation of specialized skill consultants and out-sourced process operations have naturally had a significant influence in the way 'help seeker' organizations view the growth of their internal capabilities in analytics. Many decision makers have felt that building a specialized analytics operations within the firm with statistical and computation specialist capability will be ideal for the analytics journey. Our view is that, for most companies with fragmented information sources (which form the majority of organizations), such specialization in an evolving environment will not yield satisfactory results.

In a later chapter of this book, we shall describe our study of select India-based organizations in their attempts to adopt business analytics to support their decision-making process. Some of these issues discussed here appear to be very pertinent for organizations in the Indian context.

How Has the Perception of Analytics Transformed Over Time?

Many years ago, one of the authors faced an unenviable situation when the senior management of a respectable private sector bank contended that analytical tools would have little relevance to their enterprise in the long run. The bank was profitable by servicing the creamy segment of the society and barring creativity and impeccable relationship management skills, it did not require much to maintain its business.

Unfortunately, for many such enterprises, the world has moved on in the intervening period and Analytics has become an inevitable option. To their credit, many such organizations changed their focus admirably by adapting to the new requirements of data science (liberally substituted for Analytics) in a prudent and timely manner to avoid any significant downturn in their performance.

The current data science revolution is seemingly passing through a phase of extreme positive euphoria, almost like it is perceived to be the 'manna' from heaven that provides the next generation of resolutions to business problems.

Needless to state, both these extreme sentiments cited previously are improper representation of the true value of this science to organizations. Hopefully, this euphoria will be replaced over time by a more practical but useful perception of its role as a pervasive 'ether' in the organization, supporting and guiding all decision making, yet not getting in the way of common sense acumen. Such embedded representation is the true example of an evolved business enterprise thriving on the power of information management that Analytics can fuel in the long run.

We want to bring out another dimension to the discussion on analytics. No discussion on analytics today can end without some prognosis on the impact of the newest opportunity in the domain: BIG DATA. We had made a brief mention of the same earlier in the chapter. Our intention is not to delve into a detailed discussion of its impact on business and our life style in general. Rather, we intend to keep our discussion on analytics at a more general level avoiding any specificity. There are optimists resting high hopes on the potential of Big

Data to bring revolutionary changes in every aspect of our life like what internet did starting in 1970. On the other hand, the sceptics have a feeling that it may eventually be proved to be a 'big dud'. The challenge that 'Big Data' analytics faces is mainly to extract meaningful pattern or correlations from unstructured data which is exploratory in nature. On the other hand, the amount of information (insight) such data contains is possibly a miniscule part of it and most of it is just noise. With more data deluge and at a faster pace, the noise may be increasing faster than the signal. Finding a pattern in it is like searching a needle in a haystack. Consequently, the chances of false discoveries of patterns are increasing by leaps and bounds. Eventually, it is the deep knowledge in the domain that could avert such a catastrophic situation. Hence, like every other nascent discovery, we would advise an open but objective view of the potential value that this information source may bring to society.

What to Look Forward to in this Book?

You may be worried about the magnitude of information and resources, processes and tactical initiatives that are described in the Analytics domain, without anyone providing an overall direction as to how such capabilities need to be directed to achieve business goals. How do you make your investment in Analytics work for you? Should you invest in Analytics infrastructure and specialists and let them drive the process? These are vexing questions with no clear answers.

While we may not have specific solutions to your dilemma, the rest of this book is meant to address such concerns to the extent a book can possibly do. It deals primarily with assisting business leaders (with or without current investments in analytics operations) decide on how they should drive their analytics initiatives in their organizations. Although there

Figure I.3 The Analytics Process

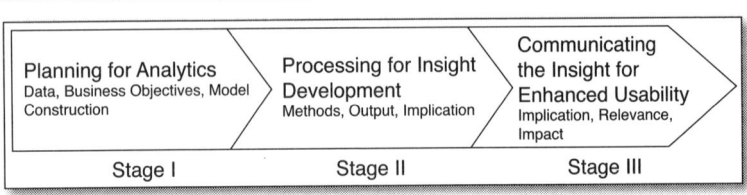

Planning for Analytics Data, Business Objectives, Model Construction	Processing for Insight Development Methods, Output, Implication	Communicating the Insight for Enhanced Usability Implication, Relevance, Impact
Stage I	Stage II	Stage III

is no golden rule to be applied (which is why the problem is a trifle complex), a few logically sequenced 'good' practices and 'thinking points' can help many organizations get better payoffs for their investment in this foray. We refer to the Analytics Process (Figure I.3), to illustrate the discussions in the subsequent chapters.

The next chapter will discuss the approach to creating a data map of the organization, which connects elemental pieces of business/organizational data to their potential use in answering questions of relevance to the business (Stage I). Without such a guide map, analytic ventures may look hollow and disconnected with the requirements of the business. It serves the purpose of lending direction to the firm in terms of where, what and how useful analysis may be performed.

In a subsequent chapter (Chapter 2), we shall address the issue of connecting some data analytic problems (and models) to their actual role in addressing a business problem (Stage II). We shall categorize different forms of data-driven analysis and describe their end goals. Basis our high-level understanding of data analysis methods, we shall also specifically look at 'how business managers should spell out realistic goals for analytics projects' and how then can they monitor success and failure of the same (Chapter 3). We believe these are two major dimensions on which business leaders should gain knowledge to better communicate their requirements to technical resources in organizations who manage the analytics projects (Stage I). Conversely, these are useful capabilities for technicians in the Analytics domain to effectively communicate the value of their output to their consumers (decision makers) in the organizations. We shall then provide some guidelines on communicating Analytic results (Stage III) in a logical manner to add value to the decision-making process (Chapter 4). This, in our understanding, is one of the weakest links in making analytics effective in organizations. The producers (analysts) and consumers (decision makers) of analytic output many times speak in different languages not discernible to one another.

Finally, we shall end Part I of this book with a commentary (Chapter 5) on the existing Analytic infrastructure that is available for organizations to invest in, to ramp up their analytics output. It will also provide an approach to evaluate such investment decisions. We have deliberately kept this chapter towards the end of Part I of the book to emphasize the importance of planning analytics capability well, before evaluating infrastructure needs that support the capability.

1

Where to Begin: Managing Organization's Data Inventory for Effective Decision Support

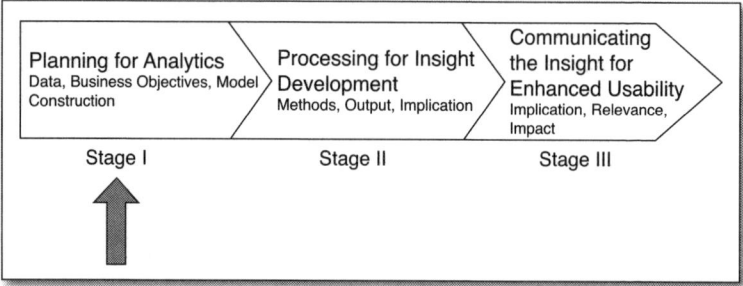

Planning for Analytics Data, Business Objectives, Model Construction	Processing for Insight Development Methods, Output, Implication	Communicating the Insight for Enhanced Usability Implication, Relevance, Impact
Stage I	Stage II	Stage III

*B*ipin Swamy, the Chief Executive Officer of a mid-sized consumer durables company, recently attended a highly rated conference on 'Analytics and its Usage in Business Applications' at Bangalore. He had specifically attended the conference to pick-up leads on how he should drive his company's Analytics investments in line with the needs of the company in the near future. The conference was a huge success with experts in the industry presenting the various trends, tools and technology available to facilitate Analytics practices in organizations.

Somehow, Bipin felt that while the information available in the seminars and workshops at the conference were useful, he came back somewhat unsure about what may be a useful starting point for conceptualizing his near term Analytics plan for the firm. An approach note on how to evaluate the organizational information inventory that could be structured for better decision support use was something not discussed at all at the conference. He wondered how Analytics conferences seemed to focus on tools and data platforms, but no one talked about tacit elements like organizational data strategy—something that was an essential building block towards creating effective data analytic platform in an organization.

Bipin's problem, however, is not unusual at many organizations. A significantly large number of organizations have invested in elaborate data platforms and analytical tool boxes only to discover that they lack the necessary know how about what is useful analysis and how data might be analysed for a specific purpose. Therefore, it is very necessary to have a clear starting point to define a productive Analytics investment in an organization. Just to ensure connect with the stages of an analytics process (referred in Introduction) and reproduced at the top of this page, we are addressing the issues of 'Planning'.

The first step towards useful analysis (productive analytics) is to get a good understanding on the availability of data to the organization and its 'true' value for decision making. Here we mean not just taking stock of the inventory of facts that is banked in the organization but also an assessment of its necessity as inputs in certain decision-making processes. This chapter focuses on how to decide/identify the value of the information that is available in the organization, and also on the criticality of information that is unavailable to decision makers.

How Should Decision Makers Look at Data Audit?

The first question to ask is, what do I need data for, rather what decisions do I need to take (either ongoing or just once) that require support with data. This may be the first step towards linking decision making to specific and relevant analysis.

Usually, this step is easy since most decision makers probably know (or they should) what support they require for and what calls they may have to take. Obviously, this part cannot be outsourced. However, the next step is to break the problem into more elementary sub decision parts that collectively feed into the overall decision problem that needs resolution. This process is repeated to explode the overall problem all the way to elemental dimensions that can be researched separately (or in groups, as the case may be). The emphasis is on progressively exploding the overall problem into parts that are relatively manageable in terms of finding answers. At the same time, it is expected that the sum of the elements add up to comprehensively address the problem as a whole. A hierarchical structure of this type is depicted in Figure 1.1.

The advantage of this exercise is that it links up higher level organizational decision-making issues in a hierarchical manner to all the disaggregated constituent analyses that support the overall decision-making process. In the process the planning of analysis and identification of data requirement is done systematically to ensure that all the dimensions of the problem to be resolved are addressed (the bottom most box in Figure 1.1 identifies the data and its sources).

To be able to reinforce this idea, let's consider an example. The decision maker has to review the viability of setting up a new business. (See Appendix 1 for a business case in which this problem is relevant.) As a consultant problem solver to the decision maker, you will agree that the viability

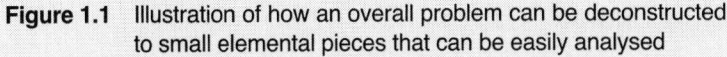

Figure 1.1   Illustration of how an overall problem can be deconstructed to small elemental pieces that can be easily analysed

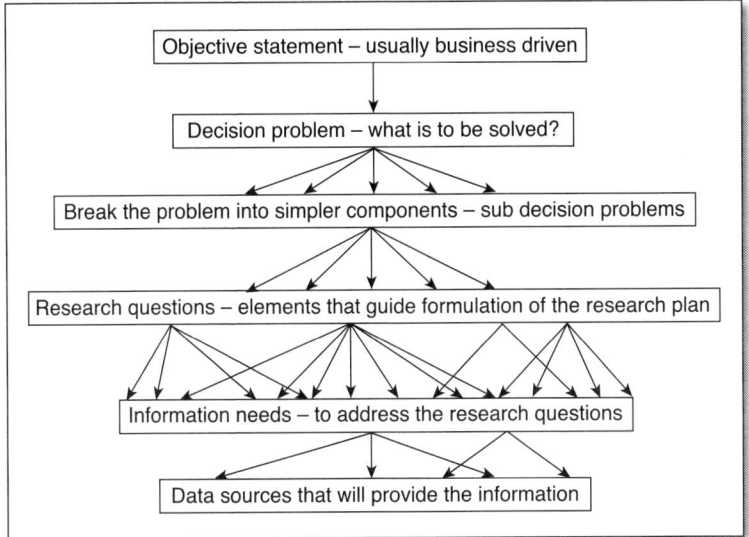

assessment would require answers to many questions such as, (a) opportunity sizing, (b) profiling of customers and ability to access them, (c) description of the product or service to be offered, (d) pricing of the service, (e) the design of the service model and the cost of developing the same, (f) added measures to be taken for contingencies, if any and (g) any other pertinent issue related to the context.

Each of these dimensions are individual pieces (if not independent) that are related to and support the final decision to (or not to) go ahead with a business proposition. Concurrently, each of these dimensions may require their own separate analysis with an identified set of information and sourcing of the same. This can be depicted as part of the planning of this viability study in the form of a 'horizontal' tree as depicted in Figure 1.2.

The important point to be noted is that the hierarchical 'blow up' in Figure 1.2 is able to link the 'Decision Problem'

Figure 1.2 Illustration of a Viability Study Planning

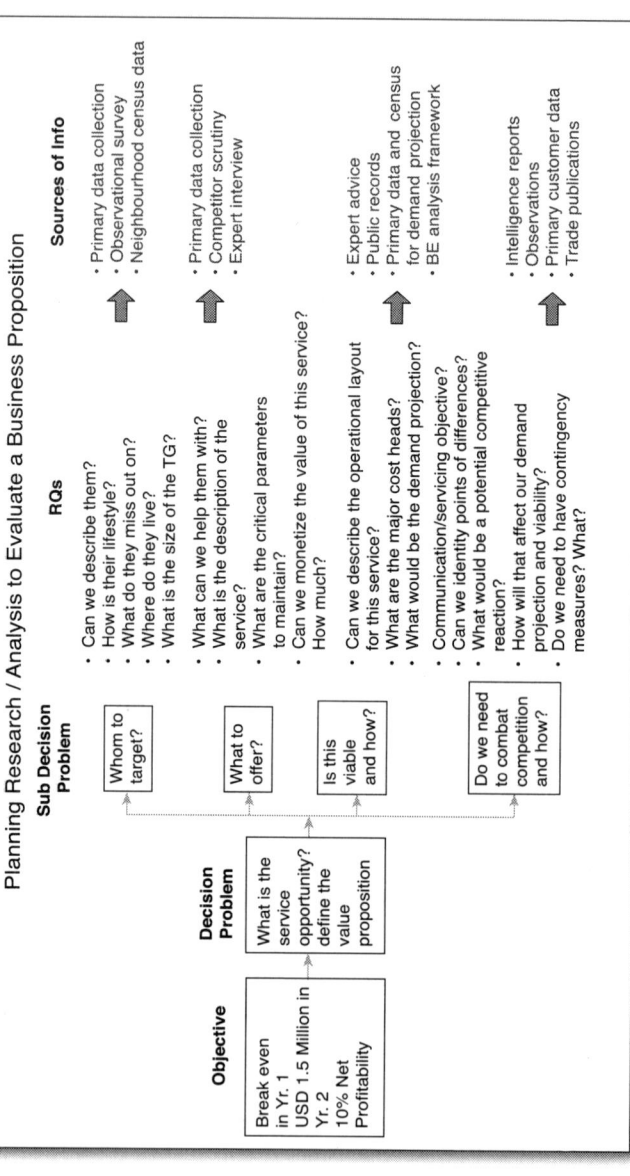

Planning Research / Analysis to Evaluate a Business Proposition

Objective	Decision Problem	Sub Decision Problem	RQs	Sources of Info
Break even in Yr. 1 USD 1.5 Million in Yr. 2 10% Net Profitability	What is the service opportunity? define the value proposition	Whom to target?	Can we describe them? How is their lifestyle? What do they miss out on? Where do they live? What is the size of the TG?	Primary data collection Observational survey Neighbourhood census data
		What to offer?	What can we help them with? What is the description of the service? What are the critical parameters to maintain? Can we monetize the value of this service? How much?	Primary data collection Competitor scrutiny Expert interview
		Is this viable and how?	Can we describe the operational layout for this service? What are the major cost heads? What would be the demand projection? Communication/servicing objective? Can we identity points of differences?	Expert advice Public records Primary data and census for demand projection BE analysis framework
		Do we need to combat competition and how?	What would be a potential competitive reaction? How will that affect our demand projection and viability? Do we need to have contingency measures? What?	Intelligence reports Observations Primary customer data Trade publications

and the 'Objective' to the elemental dimensions (Sub Decisions and Research Questions) and further to the 'sources of information' that would provide inputs to address each of the issues identified. In this way, the analyst and the decision maker are able to comprehend how individual pieces of analysis are useful for the final resolution of the business problem. This is an example of a comprehensive documentation of a plan to resolve a problem.

Whereas in reality, most analysts may be comfortable framing Research Questions (RQs) and initiating analysis and research based on the identified questions, there are some visible limitations in this practice. It is hard to ascertain if the identified set of research questions are exhaustive to address the problem comprehensively. Hence, it is necessary to link it up logically to the end objective (the definition of the problem).

While there is no compulsion, it may be noted that the discipline of linking RQs back to the business problem ensures, (a) an effective communication stream to the decision maker or consumer of the research and analysis and, (b) ensures that there is comprehensiveness in the analyses and that all relevant research/analysis dimensions are accounted for. Effective communication is usually a useful method to ensure that analysis and research are valued by the decision makers.

To illustrate the above point further, we take the example of our experience with a large retail bank in the United States that had hired one of us (as a part of a consulting team) to help transform their business. The bank had suffered losses in one of its key business lines (private label credit card) and wanted assistance in identifying opportunities to restore its profitability.

After several rounds of contextual deep dives, the team offered a 'road map' to address the issue of turnaround for the bank (Figure 1.3). It is apparent from the structure of

Figure 1.3 Research Matrix for a Business Turnaround Project

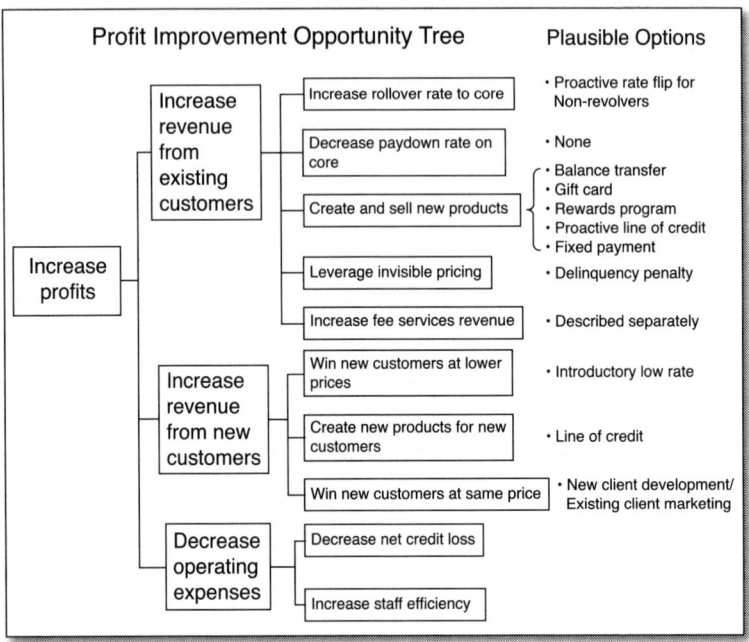

the 'tree' that the objective behind the research (Increasing Profits) was progressively 'exploded' to identify potential opportunities areas and link them in a hierarchical manner to specific initiatives. For instance, 'Increasing Overall Profits' could be attained through either 'Increasing revenues from existing customers' or 'Revenue opportunities from new customers' or 'Decreasing operating expenses'. The important point to note is that the opportunities were 'exploded' such that mutually exclusive categories were identified and yet, all together they comprehensively addressed all the opportunities towards attaining the final objective (increasing profits). Similarly, the next levels of options were identified and placed adopting the same rule of 'mutually exclusive but collectively exhaustive' categories. This was done until individual initiatives (for example, Balance Transfer, Gift Cards,

Delinquency Penalty, etc.) could be identified that required separate evaluation to ascertain if there was an opportunity to increase profit by initiating them.

In the process, the research and consulting team ensured that all potential (and identified) opportunities for 'Improving Profits' were unravelled for the bank. Once the scope of analysis was identified, the bank and its advisors could decide which initiatives to analyse to explore their potential.

This exercise provided a basis for realizing the potential set of analyses that could be performed to realize profit for the bank. Theoretically, the 'tree' should be extended (to the right) to include data requirements for the analysis of each of the initiative. However, in this case, it was ignored since the data requirements were obvious to all stakeholders. Additionally, readers may note that we have digressed from the original rule of connecting business question to research questions and instead identified analysis of initiatives that may accomplish our business objective. Usually, this is appropriate as long as the philosophy of connecting the overall objective to individual strands of analysis is maintained.

Contextual Familiarity—Multiple Perspectives of the Problem

The discipline of building such analyses tree is certainly an important trait to realize, but the primary requirement for building a good data plan in an organization is the necessity to identify the right issues impacting it. If the problem definition is erroneous, the rest of the research tree is certainly an irrelevant exercise. To be able to identify the right issues, problem solvers need to be able to grasp the essence of the business realities. Often times, perception regarding the true problem (issues) facing the organization may vary across different stakeholders. For one, they are perhaps looking at the problem from their own perspective. Usually, for the problem solver, in such a situation, it is worthwhile to 'absorb' as many perspectives of the problem as possible from multiple members of the decision-making body to be able to identify the crux of the issues that the organization faces. It helps to formulate one's own perspective about the problem(s) based on assimilating multiple perspectives and then presenting to the decision-making body the synthesis of the same. Usually in this process, the real issues are identified and a general agreement is reached about what is important. It is important to be able to perform this process diligently in order to build an effective analytics/research plan for the organization in the long run. Let us consider an example to substantiate this point:

A tyre manufacturing unit supplying largely to industrial buyers engaged a consultant to evaluate the prospect of enhancing the market presence of the company in the replacement market (direct to consumer). (See Appendix 2 for a detailed description of the business case.) The consultant met with many stakeholders of the organization including the president of the unit, the marketing manager and some distributors of tyres in the replacement market along with other relevant functionaries and proposed a research project to the top management which would potentially evaluate the viability of entering (enhancing the presence in) the replacement market and the entry strategy to be adopted.

This proposal, after the initial approvals were taken, was presented to the owner of the tyre unit (Managing Director). On hearing the proposal, the owner emphatically disagreed with the objective. Her view was that the organization was not interested in entering the replacement market in a significant way. Instead, she wanted to know if her industrial buyers (manufacturers of vehicles) may turn away in the long run, unless she created a known 'brand' in the minds of the end consumer. She was worried that her current clients were already putting pressure on her unit to reduce selling price, since her products were largely unknown to their customers and hence it was getting difficult for them to sell their vehicles with this tyre.

What emerged out of this discussion was that the intended research was not about evaluating the 'viability of getting into the replacement market' but had to do with a different problem: 'is the firm being forced to enter the replacement market to save their current business model of selling to industrial buyers and if so, with what consequence'.

Clearly, most stakeholders had a different perception about the true problem (or interpretation of the problem) than the owner. Finally, the multiple perspectives were discussed and the collectively agreed upon problem statement was arrived, which formed the basis on which the research was conducted. With more clarity and congruence among business stakeholders, this process can be made more efficient. But in reality, that is rarely achieved.

The Criticality of 'Good' Data Resource

Investing in data resources that are meaningful for business decision making is a critical task for most astute organizational leaders. There is no substitute for it. Unlike a somewhat popular perception that analytical methods can extract insights useful for organizations, it may be noted that methods only facilitate the extraction of the insights available in 'good' data resources, but they do not substitute for the latter. Hence, a crucial task for organizations is to audit data requirements based on their needs for various decision support, as described in the previous sections, and ensure availability of the same either by developing appropriate data capture and/or by data management procedures. 'Good' data ensures (a) better insights, (b) better prediction and (c) better inferencing.

Many analysts and decision makers perceive that utilizing more sophisticated methodology to extract insights will be helpful when more basic methods fail. Barring a few stray instances, this perception is largely unfounded. Hence, it is necessary to realize the strategic role that data quality plays in building healthy analytics-driven business processes.

Does Bipin Swamy Have a Plan to Work On?

Bipin is well advised to prescribe the following approach to his organization:

1. Identify and define issues that require inputs (information) and,
2. To 'explode' the issues into simpler sub parts that facilitate ease of analyses.

We term this as a good investment of business acumen prior to the more significant investment in tools and techniques with significant financial implication. It is an investment in a disciplined approach to solving problems which is hard to perfect. But, it has long lasting impact on effective data-driven decision-making climate in organizations. Without this discipline, research processes in organizations may be relegated to a non-critical function with minimal value (perceived necessity but with no measured value output). Bipin's team has work cut out for them, before they worry about specific analyses.

To leverage the potential of the data inventory in your organization, you may want to familiarize yourself with the types of analyses that can be done. The next chapter provides an exposition of the major categories of analyses that are done in practice and their intended purpose. Necessary data forms that support these analyses will also be discussed. We will delve into this in the chapter on tool box appreciation (part of Stage II in our Analytics Process discussed earlier).

2

Useful Approaches to Mining Information: Building Intuition of Analytic Tools

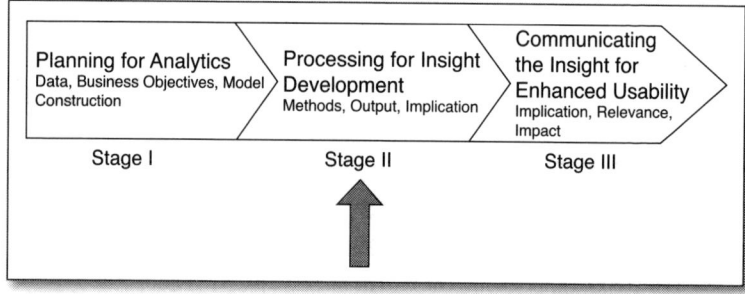

*S*arita Singh (Sarita), a business head of a mid-sized apparel manufacturing firm with sales in both domestic and international market needed an appreciation of the kind of analyses she could do with her sales and customer level data. While she understood that business analyses eventually had to be tailored based on her business questions for which she wanted answers, she was not sure what may be the best way to frame her specific questions in line with the way the analyst would work with the data. Hence, a broader view of the kinds of analyses that numeric data can be used for would really help her appreciate the power *of data processing better. She hoped that someone could explain to her the various ways (broadly) that data could be viewed to obtain potentially useful insight.*

The above vignette summarizes the confusion that many business managers have about how to visualize what a data analytics project may yield. While the onus of finding answers to business questions may lie with the analyst, as consumers of information insights, business managers would appreciate a broad understanding of the ways data can be processed, which helps them plan their analyses better. This chapter is an attempt to do just that.

What we are about to describe are the basic elements of processing tools that an analyst will work with in Stage II of a typical Analytical process (described earlier). Detailed understanding of tools and methodology are outside the scope of this book.

Introduction

The basic source of information is data. While data may appear in many forms, for this exposition, we shall limit the definition of data largely to structured data (numeric data is an example). Unstructured data or text data, while it is an increasingly important component of contemporary analytics, will not be within the primary scope of this discussion.

Structured data come in different forms—qualitative data and quantitative data. Most qualitative and quantitative data follow a scale of measurement. Qualitative data will usually be in nominal (categorical) and ordinal scale (ordered/ranked). Quantitative data comes in interval scale (the difference between two values can be compared across in the order of magnitude with other difference) or, ratio scale (Absolute values can be compared on order of magnitude). The value of information residing in different scales varies and is associated with the nature of the scale. Nominal data have the least amount of information (identifies unique categories of entities), ordinal scale has a bit more (identifies separable entities and also orders them in ascending or descending order), interval and ratio scales have the maximum amount of information, conducive for extracting information through sophisticated analysis, but usually these scales are harder to apply and to collect from respondents because of their evolved characteristics. More on measurement scales can be accessed in any basic book on research methodology.

Categorizing Analyses

It is hard to categorize analytical procedures. Nevertheless, observation of different practices reveals that they can be bracketed largely into three kinds: (a) Predictive Analytics, (b) Exploratory or Identification Analytics and (c) Normative Analytics. The first two categories fall under the 'discovery' mode while the last one is meant to provide guidance to management on 'what to do' based on building a business model on information.

1. PREDICTIVE ANALYTICS

This is a family of analysis driven largely to identify influencers/drivers/association variables of a particular target response variable(s). This is usually employed to understand how the variation in a business performance metric is influenced by 'driver' variables that can be manipulated by managers. The common approach to build predictive models is to identify a target response variable which is usually associated with a critical business performance parameter. The model-building exercise tries to associate the target variable to other exogenous business parameters which are presumably controllable by the mangers. With changes in the external variables (controllable by the managers), the model is able to estimate the probable change in the target variable level. As a consequence, predictive models are appealing to most decision makers since they act as a precursor to deciding on best strategies.

Predictive models are built with two kinds of target variables: continuous (interval scaled) variables and categorical variables (see Figure 2.1). Models with continuous target variables (sale volume, profits, revenue, etc.) are usually based on a statistical procedure known as the linear regression. Categorical variable models are generically built using logistic regression. But irrespective of the nature of the target variable, the philosophy of model building remains the same—associate a relevant target variable to its 'driver' variables.

Figure 2.1   Predictive Analytics–Separation Algorithms

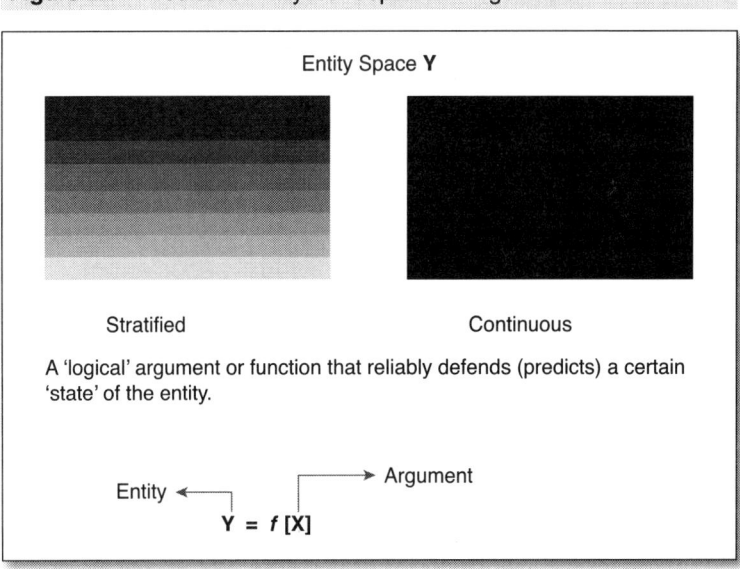

In Sarita's case (see vignette at the beginning), if she would like to understand what are the drivers of sales (target) for a particular type of apparel, she may want to associate the apparel type (design, material colour), its price and any other relevant variable to their impact on sales. If she has data on these variables strung together (over time), she would like to know what is (are) causing the variation in the sales. Her objective may be very well addressed using a predictive model.

A practical example of such a prediction model is the Marketing Mix Model, which is prolifically used in consumer goods industry to evaluate success of marketing initiatives in the past year. The model results provide a good input into the planning exercise for marketing activities in the next planning cycle. Here, sales volume of a brand/product/ category of products is regressed over data on various marketing activities to evaluate their effectiveness (the estimated regression coefficients are a good indicator of the influence of the mix variable).

The approach used in such regression-based models is depicted in Figure 2.2. A fast moving consumer goods (FMCG) marketing firm wants to identify the drivers of its 'sales' of a brand. Various marketing mix variables (price, advertising and promotion) are juxtaposed on 'sales' to see if there is association in the changes in the sales with changes in these 'mix' variables. Many times, it is impossible to see the association by simply eyeballing the data and a computation algorithm is used to extract the individual associations.

The advantage of this extraction procedure is that it identifies the influence of each marketing mix variables on the outcome (sales). Planning managers at this FMCG firm may use this information to identify which variables to manipulate (and how much) to favourably influence sales of their products. A detailed illustration of this model is presented in the Appendix 3. Appendix 3A provides a description of the statistical model (regression) that drives this analysis.

Figure 2.2   Regression Models–An Example

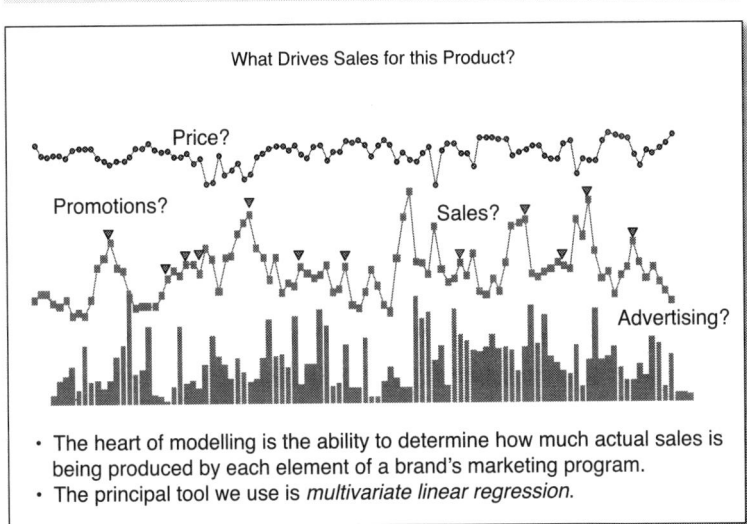

What Drives Sales for this Product?

Price?

Promotions?

Sales?

Advertising?

- The heart of modelling is the ability to determine how much actual sales is being produced by each element of a brand's marketing program.
- The principal tool we use is *multivariate linear regression*.

Nominally scaled (categorical) target variables are used to measure behaviour such as customer churn (stay/leave), profitability (profitable/unprofitable), delinquency behaviour (will default repayment/will not default), etc.

Usually, customer characteristics and past behaviour are used as predictor variables to evaluate the propensity of observing a certain target behaviour pattern in the future. These models are generically known as 'logistic regression models', although a wide variety of closely associated methods can be used to build them as well. The models are similar to the regression models described previously (see Figure 2.3). They identify associations between the target variable (which is binary in this case and depicted in different colours) and antecedent variable. Wherever the identified association is strong, the antecedent variable is considered to be an important explanatory variable for the target (variable) level. Usually, these models are used in practice to define profiles of customers (high risk versus low risk, profitable versus

Figure 2.3   Logistic Regression–Basis of Estimation

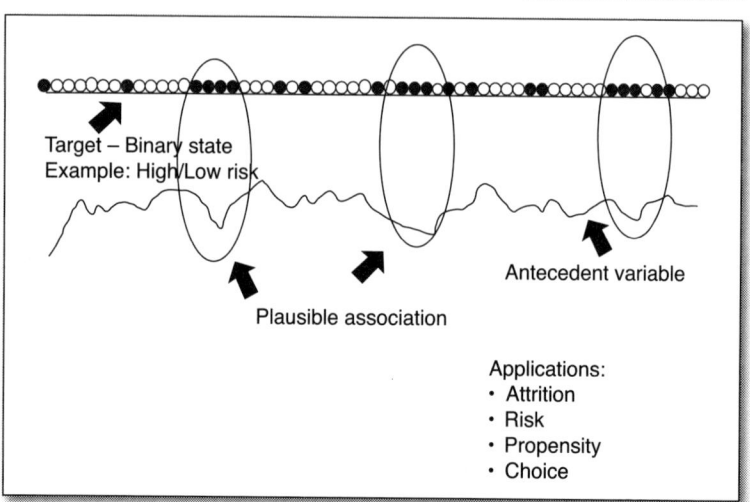

not-so-profitable customers, will choose the brand versus will not choose the brand) on some physical characteristics (demographic) variables or past behaviour.

The closest relevance of these models to Sarita's interest could be if she wanted to know what drives the choice (by the customer) of a certain brand of apparel. Here the target variable would be choice (Yes/No) of the brand of interest and the driver variables could be same as we have described earlier.

See Appendix 4 for a more detailed description of these (propensity) models.

2. EXPLORATORY OR IDENTIFICATION ANALYTICS

The objective of finding associations among variables remains as before for this family of analysis. However, a chief difference between Predictive Analytics and Exploration is that, in the latter there is no central theme or target variable whose association with other variables is projected.

In Exploratory Analytics, all associations are identified (in numeric terms through a correlational analysis or other measures of closeness among variables). The final discovery is a determination based on a scientific measure of closeness and also the suitability of the information to the analyst's decision-making requirements (see Figure 2.4). Segmentation analysis (for example, cluster analysis) and dimension reduction (factor analysis) are some of the more popular techniques used for Exploratory Analytics.

Exploration is a process that falls midway between an application of science and the artistic dexterity of the analyst. Careful observation of the data, forming impressions of the

Figure 2.4 Separation Algorithms–Exploratory

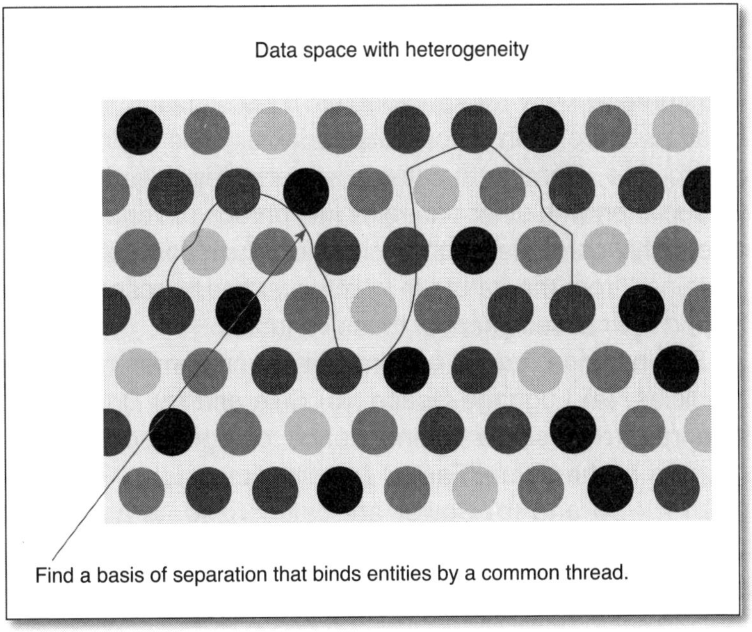

Data space with heterogeneity

Find a basis of separation that binds entities by a common thread.

information based on newer discoveries of associations and applying right judgement are the required traits of a data analyst for making superior inferencing from the data. New age techniques of text mining and sentiment analysis use a concept of similarity index which conceptually is similar to a correlation analysis described here.[1]

We must emphasize here that many times exploratory analysis will not follow a standard set of rules and norms. Instead, as discussed earlier, the approach is quasi-scientific and has a large judgemental component. It develops as newer insights are revealed from the data. Domain knowledge is critical for applying the appropriate judgement calls. Hence, for more insightful exploratory analysis, the data analyst and the business leader need to actively work in a collaborative manner.

Box 2.1 provides an example output of exploratory Factor Analysis that is conducted to group variables (dimensions) on which products/brands/goods are rated, into broader categories based on the similarity in the way respondents (customers) view these variables. This similarity is measured as correlation among the variables. The factor analysis routine attempts to categorize variables based on their association with other variables into groups of variables that are highly correlated with each other. Such correlations are obtained from the nature in which customers (respondents) report their assessment of these variables.

For instance, based on similarity in customer ratings of vehicles, (a) Luggage Space, (b) Size and (c) Roominess are regarded similarly and hence categorized together as part of the same 'Factor' (macro dimension). Similarly, (a) Pick-Up and (b) Power are categorized as a different

---

[1] For a detailed explanation of standard correlations-based exploratory analysis, readers may refer to J. Hair, R. Anderson, R. Tatham, and W. Black, *Multivariate Data Analysis*, 5th ed. (NJ, USA: Prentice Hall Inc., 1998).

Box 2.1 Example of Exploratory Factor Analysis

Automobile research foundation (ARF) conducted research on customer preferences for automobiles on multiple relevant evaluation criteria (nine variables) for automobiles. In order to ascertain if all these dimensions were independently useful, they decided to ask customers for the importance rating of each of these variables. Using the importance rating scores of a customer sample, they conducted Factor Analysis to see if the variable were associated with each other.

The Analysis results showed that there are three broad categories of variables: (a) Pick-Up and Power, (b) Size, Luggage Space and Roominess and (c) Gas mileage and Maintenance Cost. The categories (Factors 1, 2 and 3) are identified below and their association with the original variables are given in terms of Factor Loadings. Price, Seating Capacity and Operating Costs seem to have more 'diffused' association with multiple categories (based on their Factor Loadings, usually between ±1)

Percentage of Total Variance Explained

1	2	3
33.976	13.141	9.527

Rotated Loading Matrix (VARIMAX, Gamma = 1.0000)

Factors→ Variables ↓	1	2	3
Pick-up	0.139	0.105	0.641
Power	0.100	0.109	0.772
Size	0.780	0.165	0.094
Luggage Space	0.720	−0.123	0.274
Seating Capacity	0.431	0.025	0.570
Roominess	0.702	0.281	0.166
Operating Cost	0.031	0.583	0.462
Price	0.301	0.295	0.455
Gas mileage	−0.009	0.807	0.178
Maintenance Costs	0.255	0.745	−0.023

Note: Factor Loading closer to 1 or −1 infer higher association.

'Factor' given that they are similar to each other based on correlations (Factor loadings give an indication of the similarity of the variable with a Factor, closer to 1 or −1 means higher association). Some variables however, do not have a firm association with any category, for instance, Price, Operating Cost and Seating capacity.

Factor Analysis provides a platform to reduce data without a commensurate reduction in the information content of the data. Using correlation as the basis of commonality across variables, it clubs variables with similar 'information' and bunches them together (each one of the variables represents others). In applications, this is a useful way to summarize the information into tighter dimensions, helpful for understanding and interpreting the information.

Going back to Sarita, she may be curious to know more about her customers' preferences of apparels. For instance, she may like to group the dimensions on which she feels customers base their purchases into broader and lesser number categories (based on how similar they are perceived by customers). This would enable her to understand purchase drivers better. Such objectives can be met by running Factor Analysis described previously.

She may also like to group customers based on their purchases (if she has tracked purchase data of her regular customers). She could bunch them into homogenous groups (segments) on the basis of the commonality of their purchases. Then, she could look at their description (who they are?), to describe them better and link that to their purchases. That may give her leads about how she could focus on selling her goods to the right customers in the future (part of the overall customer relationship management strategies that organizations follow). Hence, a lot of analyses can be done to yield useful insights, provided of course the data is available.

More information on the utility of the Factor Analysis and other forms of Exploratory Analysis are presented in standard textbooks on 'Research Methodology for Business Applications'.

3. NORMATIVE ANALYTICS

What price should I set for my product? How much should I spend on advertising support for my product? Do I need to back it up with local area promotions?

Optimization techniques are used to provide ideal answers to such questions. The objective function in a normative model is usually constructed based on a predictive model for a target variable performance measure (see Figure 2.5).

The driver parameters (often times marketing variables) are manipulated within a reasonable range (dictated by organizational resource constraints and other external factors) to identify the corresponding expected business performance (based on the estimate of the response variable). Among all

Figure 2.5   Normative Analytics–What Should I do?

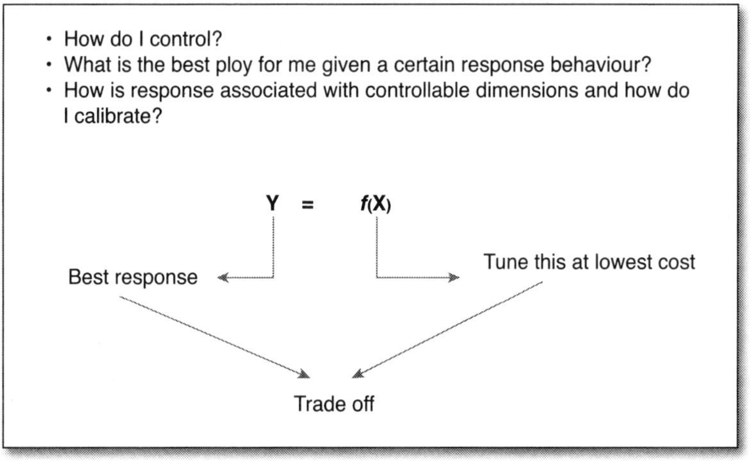

- How do I control?
- What is the best ploy for me given a certain response behaviour?
- How is response associated with controllable dimensions and how do I calibrate?

$$Y = f(X)$$

Best response

Tune this at lowest cost

Trade off

types of analysis, this category appeals to decision makers the most for its prescriptive nature of the output. These are also called 'What If' scenario analyses, since they provide the flexibility to evaluate multiple hypothetical scenarios. However, it must be noted that in most cases the output is perhaps an imperfect representation of an effective prescription (because of the constraints with most models being an imperfect representation of reality) and hence the antidote provided needs to be taken with adequate caution.

As an example, if sales volume of a certain brand is seen to be dependent on the price discounting, advertising and promotional spending done to support it (and also competitive ploys), the brand planner's problem is to determine what should be the optimal spending in each category of the marketing mix to maximize sales volume, of course with some thought about competitive manoeuvres. If budget is not a constraint, then the optimal spending will be infinite. A budget constraint will 'force' the model to allocate marketing support to mix elements that have maximum impact on the sales, as determined by the response elasticity measures (within a reasonable limit).

In the practicing world, 'scenario builders' are used by business planners, which are developed on the backdrop of a response function estimated using data analytics. ASSESSOR,[2] CONJOINT (for new product development), CALLPLAN, Media Mix optimizer are some of the commonly used normative models used in industry and which are built on academically rigorous frameworks.

---

[2] Refer to Gary Lilien and Arvind Rangaswamy, *Marketing Engineering*, 2nd ed. (Delhi, India: Pearson Education, 2003).

Conducting Experiments

Most analytics projects are about finding valuable insights from already available data (secondary sourced data). However, there is a practice in Analytics which is about creating/collecting data in a controlled environment (through running pilots) and using them to validate hypotheses.

Often times, such methods are employed when historical data does not have much use (more so in dynamic environments). Running pilots require setting up a controlled environment (to avoid unnecessary interference from irrelevant variables) where the response to the treatment (manipulation of interest) is collected, analysed and compared with results from a controlled 'normal' environment (also termed as 'Business As Usual'). The 'normal' environment is an exact replica of the environment where the treatment is administered, except that the treatment is not administered in this case. The difference in the responses across the treatment and the control gives a measure of the impact of the treatment. The actual analysis follows the methodology described in the section on Predictive Analytics.

Experiments (Pilots) in a 'controlled' environment run up the risk of being criticized for projecting results that may be unrealistic, given that they are conducted in a simulated condition. Hence, the design of the environment in which the experiment is run is very delicately handled to ensure that the results are attributable to the treatment effect and not an artefact of the controlled environment.

Pilots have been used in Marketing to test out the performance of new products and brands. They are called Test Marketing or Simulated Test Marketing, depending upon the environment (real or artificial) where they are conducted. Going back to Sarita's apparel business, she may consider experimentation to evaluate, for instance, 'right' pricing for her apparels, especially for new products, where there is little historical basis to fall back upon.

How to Apply the Tools in the Tool Box

We now have a starting point to understand the possible usage of Analytics for organizations. But they do not comprehensively cover all possibilities. Seasoned practitioners will have a slew of creative ways to look for information around these broad categories of Analytical tools. This looks a lot similar to gourmet cooking. There is no one formula to get the best dish. There is always the scope to 'mix and match' and many times creative recipes evolve with experience. At the same time, the approach to solve the problem is never tool centric, rather a good understanding of the problem determines the resolution path and the portfolio of tools to be used (and in what sequence).

However, Sarita may find a 'cheat sheet' on application of various analyses very useful, just to get her started on connecting her business problems with plausible analytics solutions. We provide one such illustrative (but not comprehensive) reference in Table 2.1.

But the final objective is to get to a view of the data which is appropriate, sensible and useful to business. Hence, the spirit of analytics is less about implementing scientific tools and techniques literally, but more about applying the philosophy behind the deployment of such tools to appropriately view data for useful insights. As such, business may not require data scientists as much as they require professionals who imbibe the spirit of data scientists and apply the notions in their context appropriately.

The significance of blending the contextual dimensions into a model-building exercise is dealt with in the next chapter. We describe a framework to develop business

Table 2.1   Summary of Analysis Types

Nature of Analysis	Name of Analysis	Purpose	Data Requirements
Predictive	Regression/ Logistics regression	Identify influencers (and the extent of influence) on a target variable	a) Numeric/ Categorical (Target* variable) b) Numeric– Influencers
	Automatic Interaction Detection (CART/ CHAID)	Identify Influencers (without any prior knowledge of what influences)	Numeric/ Categorical
	Machine-learning Algorithms (SVM)	Better influencer identification	Numeric
Exploratory	Factor Analysis	Dimension Reduction to Simplify Analysis	Numeric (Correlation across Dimensions)
	Cluster Analysis	Categorizing Customers (Respondents) into homogenous segments	Numeric (across multiple dimensions) for each customer
	Text Mining	Content/ Sentiment Analysis	Unstructured / Qualitative
	Visualization	Summarization	Numeric / Non Numeric
Normative	Scenario Builder	'What If' analysis	Output of Predictive Models

(Continued)

(Continued)

Nature of Analysis	Name of Analysis	Purpose	Data Requirements
	Optimizer	Compute optimal values of manipulation variables	a) Function built on manipulation variables that determines the target variable b) Constraints (boundary of manipulation)

Note: *Target Variable is usually the business dimension of interest to the manager, which s(he) would like to optimize (for example, profits, revenue, costs, etc.).

benchmarks for evaluating the success of a predictive modelling output. Once these evaluating criteria are set, the analytical challenge is to deploy the most appropriate method to surpass the benchmark. Business managers are therefore charged to set these standards for analytical technicians to achieve. That is usually a good planning protocol for organizations to develop over time.

3

Resolving Business Problems with (Predictive) Analytics: Scoping the Objectives

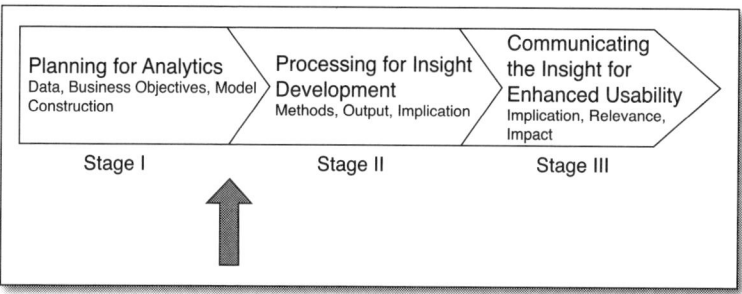

K *aran Tyagi, Marketing VP of a large consumer services company, was in conversation with his marketing intelligence support lead regarding the possibility of building a consumer response model to support his marketing campaigns. Specifically, could he ascertain how much was the monetary benefit from running the campaign using the model?*

He was keen to know from the market intelligence person whether such a model could be developed with the data available in the organization, and more importantly, how he could ascertain whether the model output was useful to him. In other words, he was worried that his intelligence support team would build a model, project the statistical superiority of the model over a naïve decision process, but he would still remain unsure if it was helpful.

He wondered if there was a way to specify what he wanted (at the minimum) from the model, so that he could see the benefit of using it. Put differently, could he have his support team translate the statistical metric of 'superiority' into a measure of business benefit which could be used to test the usefulness of the model?

How does Karan find a way to communicate his end objective for which he needs the help of a predictive model (probably!)? Can the business goal be translated into an 'Analytics' metric which then becomes the goal for the data scientist to achieve?

We specifically focus on Predictive Analytics, since it has the closest link to decision making. Many predictive models are supposedly built to forecast business outcomes (on manipulation of business parameters). Hence, the reliability of such forecasts is of utmost concern to the user of these models.

Prediction has been a much discussed and researched area in business decision making for a long time. While there have been many treatises written on this subject matter in the past, decision makers will agree that it is also necessary to distinguish between methods/tools to achieve good prediction and what should be the realistically 'good' prediction. Our feeling is that a lot of work has been written on the former, with the assumption that the latter is very contextual and may not have sound principles that can be generalized. While that may be true to an extent, it may be still worthwhile to document the generic applications where predictive analytical methods can assist in decision making and the approach that professionals can adopt to evaluate their true value.

This chapter will be helpful for marketing/business decision makers who would like to adopt predictive models for taking business decisions, but shy away from doing so because of their perceived lack of technical knowledge and which they think is required. It will also serve as a useful guide to all the modelling technologists, who would want to tweak their model-building approach to suit the appetite of their business-savvy clients (decision makers). At a broader level, it hopes to build a common platform for the technical and the business factions of the analytics domain to interact productively and plan their analyses (see inset at the top of previous page) well before launching into the technical methodology. Therefore, we are still talking about how to adopt good planning process for analytics projects. This may look a step backwards from the last chapter in terms of the stages of an analytics project. However, the reader will appreciate that without some understanding about how analytical methods work (dealt in the previous chapter), no one can plan the analysis well.

The Utopian Objective of Prediction and the Disappointment

The obvious expectation from prediction models is one of perfect prediction. 'Can I tell, for sure, what my sales are going to be next year? If not for sure, well can it be as close to it as possible?'

Every decision maker's dream would be to come as close to a perfect description of the unknown as possible, if not the perfect one. Unfortunately, many times, 'as close as possible to perfection' is not anywhere close to being good, as being perfect. Hence, it requires some reflection as to what a predictive model does to support our business systems in terms of taking the right decision.

Most analysts would attribute a less than perfect prediction condition due to leakages in prediction models. The implication of such leakage to our decision-making process needs to be studied. The starting point would be to define 'leakage', for the readers to appreciate its impact (negative mostly) to business performance. The next section does just that.

What is a Leakage in a Model?

Prediction models are meant for either (a) 'perfect' classification of respondents to pre-determined categories or (b) in the case predicting continuous outcomes to predict the exact amount. They normally use a bunch of predictor variables prefaced appropriately in a mathematical formula that computes the expected 'category for classification' or expected 'amount' (as discussed in the previous chapter). In both these instances, there will be leakages since 'all models are imperfect'.

In the case of classification problems, a leakage is defined as a wrong classification by the prediction model. The quality of the prediction output depends on the percentage of wrong classification (inversely dependent). Better models have a lower proportion of wrong classification. The challenge for most decision makers is to determine what should be the minimum percentage of wrong classification that they can tolerate. This problem has a very contextual answer and is highly dependent on the impact that the wrong classification can have on the business performance.

Similarly, in continuous outcome determination (predicting volume of sales for instance), most (or practically all) prediction come with a band of uncertainty, also known as the forecasting error band. The challenge for most business planners, who are charged by their respective organizations to forecast business volumes in the future, is that a band of uncertainty around the estimated value computed by a forecasting model is more critical than the estimate. Wider is the band, less is the importance of the estimate since the actual may be anywhere within this wide band of uncertainty (or it is expected to be).

The classical theory of probability defines expected (or estimated) value as the one that is obtained on an average if the prediction is done many times over. Decision makers, in practice, cannot use this estimate as a good measure of forecast (especially when the band of error is wide) since the actual outcome is usually a single observation rather than an average over many occasions. Unfortunately they have to 'get it right' on every single outcome in the future. Hence, a good understanding of the leakage is very essential in ascertaining its 'damaging role' in business decisions. Let us take some examples of these leakages to reiterate this important point.

Leakage in Classification Models

Let us take the case of a population with two distinct segments 'A' and 'B'. These segments could be based on similarity in individuals' characteristics (demographics, psychographics) or attitude or behaviour. A predictive model application in this context would be to use separately a set of exogenous variables associated with these individuals (and known a priori) and build a model that would use these variables (X and their values) to predict the segment in which each individual belongs ('A' or 'B'). Ideally, the expectation from a model is that each individual is perfectly classified into their true segment (see Figure 3.1). Appendix 4 (as mentioned earlier) describes a procedure that does classification based on profile variables (exogenous variables).

The separation is usually identified by a mathematical model using antecedent variables (X).

Figure 3.1   Objective of Prediction Models

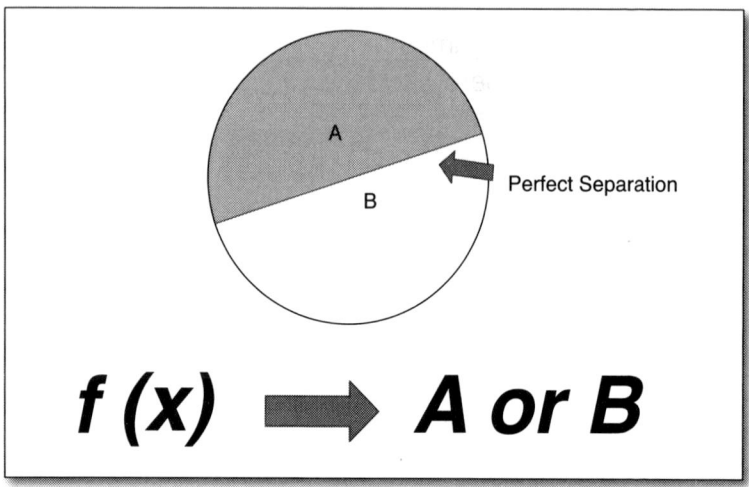

In reality, this is not achievable except in rare instances. In normal circumstances, there is bound to be some leakages—'A' classified as 'B' and vice versa (see Figure 3.2). The technical superiority of the model is judged by how small these leakages are (also reported as Confusion matrix, Gini index, ROC curve, K-S statistic etc. in technical output). The simplest statistical indicator of the quality of the model, the confusion matrix, is given as follows (Figure 3.3).

The first confusion matrix (Exact Prediction Model) shows no leakage. The total number of 'Yellow' (A) are correctly predicted since there are none that are predicted as 'White' (B) and vice versa. The off-diagonal cells, highlighted by the oval shape, provide the extent of 'bad' prediction. The second model output is more realistic where there is some leakage (or mis-classification of both 'yellow' and 'white' segments). The third model depicts close to equal proportion of correct and wrong classification. This is a case where the leakage is significant enough to render the model output useless.

Figure 3.2 Output from Actual Prediction Models

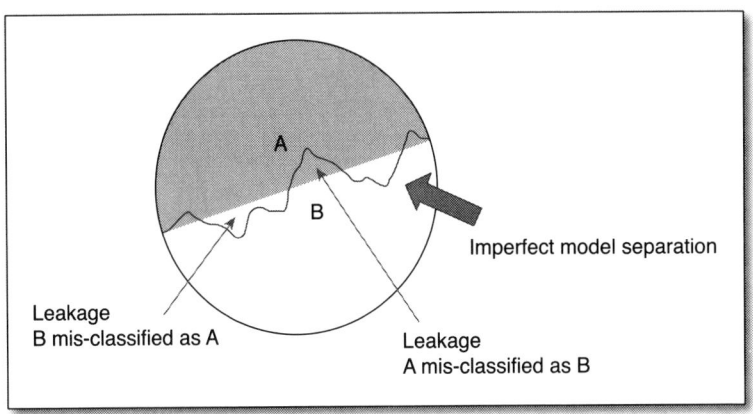

Figure 3.3 Illustrations of Confusion Matrix

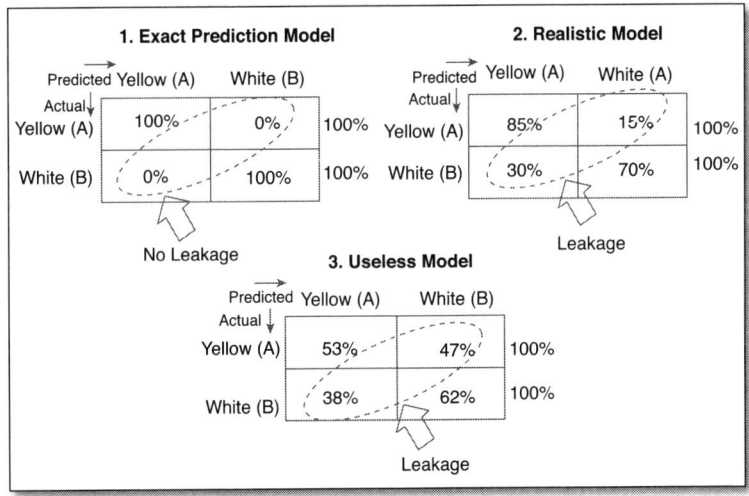

The business measure of relevance of these models depends upon how much of these leakages (and which one) can we tolerate so that the model output is still useful for decision making.

Taking a specific example, if the segment of interest to us is 'A' for a certain policy implementation but the predicted segment 'A' has on an average 30 percent of 'B' included (model output 2 in Figure 3.3), the obvious question that comes to mind is the implication of the specific policy that is being targeted on 'A' when a significant proportion of 'B' is also being inadvertently targeted with the same policy. The adverse impact of this mis-hit must be accounted for. Similarly, some members of segment 'A' (15 percent) have been erroneously classified as 'B'. Is there an adverse impact of missing out on these 'A' since they are classified as 'B'? These impacts need to be ascertained before a view is taken about the worthiness of the prediction model.

In a marketing context, often times, a segment is identified for offering additional incentives/promotions. However, with leakages of the type described previously, offering incentives to some of the wrong target segment can lead to additional costs (of subsidizing wrong target). Such costs need to be factored into the business impact model to ascertain whether the usage of the model output is indeed adding value to the firm's initiative. Specifically, it needs to be ascertained if the incremental benefit to the firm from the incentives to the target population is large enough to tide over the unnecessary cost of subsidizing (providing incentives to whom it is not meant) the wrong segment constituents due to the imperfection in the prediction model.

AYZ, a direct marketing company would like to incentivize a particular segment of customers by offering a promotional 'interest free' period for extending their usage of a retail credit facility. However, it would like to offer the discount only to the particular segment, which is expected to withdraw from the credit facility after a while and, not to others (who probably will continue anyway). Since this tendency will unravel in the future, the marketing company would like to incentivize the exact segment of customers before they make a decision to withdraw. A predictive model is usually developed to find out propensity of the customer to withdraw. Using this model, potential customers are identified based on their propensity to withdraw and the likely ones are offered the incentive. However, AYZ's problem is that if the set of 'likely' customers has a significant (though minority) proportion of 'others', it may end up targeting a significant proportion of it promotional budget to the 'wrong' customers, thereby incurring a loss. Hence, AYZ may need to assess the viability of depending on the prediction model to identify its target segment, if the target is not perfect. Specifically, the benefits of targeting the proportion of 'right' customers has to be compared with the 'loss' incurred due to targeting the proportion of 'wrong' ones and compute the net benefit. Only then can a decision to use the model can be made.

This problem is not unique to the market function. In 'People Development' function, often times extra compensation benefits are targeted to employees who are considered 'High Potential but also have a Propensity to Attrite' (HIPOPA). Organizations may not like to wait till they convey their decision to leave and hence would like to incentivize them to stay longer in the organization.

The challenge in this situation is to identify employees who are 'HIPOPA', before they reveal their intention of leaving the organization. Predictive algorithms may be used to detect in advance who fall in the target segment. However, these models have the usual leakage problems as described previously. Therefore, the model performance has to be calibrated (and measured) to ensure that the overall benefits of the incentive scheme is positive in spite of the extra cost associated with (mis)directing the scheme to a proportion of 'wrong' employees due to the imperfection in model prediction.

Another detailed example of this leakage cost in operations in the financial service domain is described in Box 3.1.

Box 3.1:   A Case on How Leakage Can Affect the Business
Performance Assessment (Experiment)

Microloan Bank

FINDING THE 'RIGHT' CREDIT DEFAULTERS TO PURSUE ARBITRATION PROCEEDINGS

Customer service managers at Microloan bank are at their wit's end trying to find the best possible way of curtailing bad debt losses which amount to over $1.8 billion annually, about 10 percent of the total balance outstanding on their VISA card. Proactive servicing of delinquent customers (those who stop paying minimum due amounts on their credit card bills) by telephone calls, letters and others means of motivating them to stay updated on their credit card payments had marginal effect on reducing the amount of bad debts.

The legal cell of Microloan bank proposed initiating arbitration proceedings against delinquent customers in order to expedite the payback process. While telephone calls and letters were milder forms of reprimanding the customer for not fulfilling their part of the obligation when they availed credit, threatening to take legal action was considered to be more aggressive and presumed to have a big impact on debt collections.

The downside of this measure was the price tag attached to initiating an arbitration procedure. For every customer on whom arbitration procedure was initiated, Microloan bank would spend $125 as arbitration fee to the National Legal Council that administered the arbitration process. This fee had to be paid regardless of the outcome of the arbitration procedure.

Collection managers at Microloan bank were reluctant to invest an additional amount of money on all defaulters in the hope that arbitration would increase the collection rate. They wanted to know how best to go about setting up the process and to send only the best prospects (customers who were most likely to pay under the threat of a legal suit) to arbitration. What they identified as the need was to find an efficient selection procedure to categorize defaulters as viable/non-viable for arbitration. This would cut down on the total cost associated with arbitration proceedings. The incremental cost would be spent only on those defaulters who were likely to pay under threat and hence the arbitration fees could be recovered from them as well. A clause in the arbitration laws in the United States required that any arbitration proceeding should be preceded by a one-month notice period, communicated by a letter from the bank to the defaulter, about the former's inclination to start arbitration if no response or payment was received from the customer during the notice period. Collection managers perceived this would be sufficient threat to motivate defaulters to act, at least the ones who would pay under threat of arbitration. The only catch to the arbitration clause was that if the letter of intent was sent, arbitration had to be followed through (which meant spending the additional $125 per case on arbitration) on every case that did not respond and pay up.

Microloan bank decided to launch a pilot study by sending a random sample of defaulters the letter informing them of possible arbitration proceedings if they did not pay up and stay current on their bills. The idea behind the pilot was to identify segments of customers, based on their characteristics available in the internal databases, who responded to the threat. MICROLOAN bank managers believed that identifying a segment of customers with a high proportion of response to the letter would help them develop an efficient selection algorithm for defaulters who are ideal candidates for arbitration. This so-called 'arbitration group' not only promises a big positive impact on dollars of debt recovered and subsequent reduction in losses due to bad debt but also guarantees minimal amount of arbitration expenditure since most of the defaulters pay up before any formal arbitration procedures are started.

The data obtained from running the pilot had the following characteristics. There were about 1500 defaulters, whose responses were tracked over a period of one month after the letters were mailed. The letters were mailed in three separate batches and the results obtained over the one-month period after the mailings were recorded. The data set contains information about who responded to the mailing and sent in at least enough money to stay current on his/her bill payment (coded as 0-non responders, 1-responders). The data set also contains information about each member of the sample collected from various internal databases at the Bank.

Figure 3.4   CART Model for Arbitration Sample

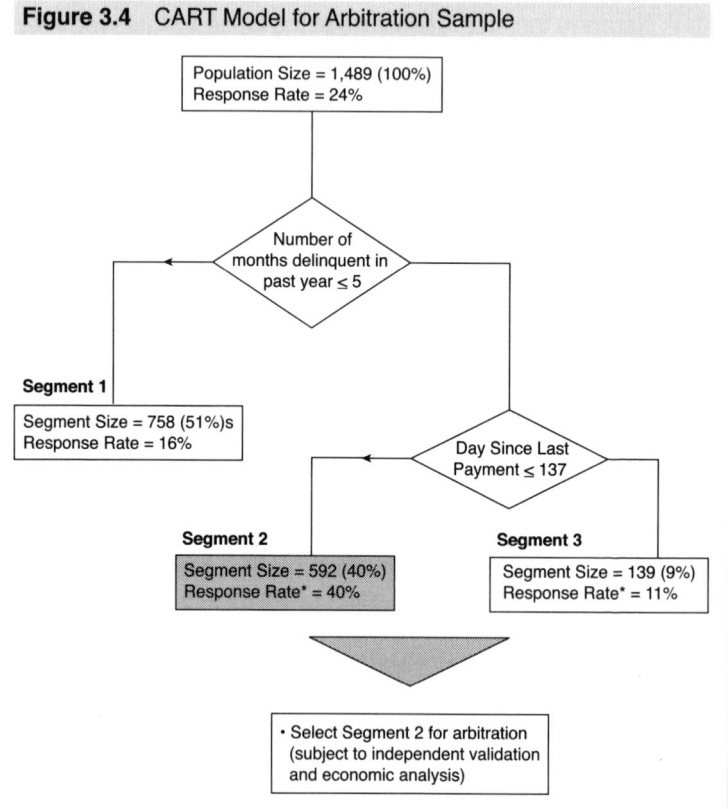

*Response is defined as paid current.

Having no hypothesis about what type of payment defaulters respond to the threat of arbitration, the analysts at the bank decided to use all the cardholder information they had, to search which dimensions were able to discriminate between responders and non-responders. The hope was that in this data exploration process some sensible segmentation variables may be identified which could be used systematically to design an efficient selection routine for arbitration (see Figure 3.4).

Based on the predictive model (CART model) on response to arbitration letter, analysts identified Segment 2 (positive response rate of 40 percent) as the prospects for sending through the arbitration process. The reason for the same is that the response in this segment was significantly higher than the average in the sample (24 percent).

However, the analysts still had to worry about the cost of sending the letter of intent to the other 60 percent non-responders in the segment 2 (leakage) in our initiative. The choice was between, (a) not sending the letter to anybody (in which case the arbitration procedure was to be put on hold) and, (b) sending letters to segment 2 identified by the antecedent variables that CART model provides.

In the latter case, analysts would have to factor the incremental response received in segment 2 to the letter (collections from 40 percent of the target), against the cost of sending the other 60 percent non-responder through the process of arbitration (and pay the application fee) with a relatively smaller possibility of recovering money from them in the long term. This cost needs to be factored to account for the model leakage that we described in the text of the paper. In case of a perfect prediction model (which would identify the 40 percent responders only), such a leakage cost would not have been factored.

Turns out that in this particular context, after factoring in the cost, the bank would still make a healthy positive collection from the initiative and hence the modelling effort was rendered successful.

Leakage in Volume Forecasting Models

These are usually regression (Ordinary Least Squares–OLS) based models that forecast continuous outcomes such as sales, revenue, cost and other business parameters that vary on a 'continuous' scale (refer Chapter 2). A set of exogenous variables are used to predict outcome through a methodology of 'best fit' of the mathematical function (of exogenous variables) to represent the outcome variable in a sample of data points, also called the training sample (see Appendix 3A for a description of Regression Models). The same function when used outside the precincts of the training sample can provide estimates of outcome for various combinations of values of exogenous variables in the future (see Figure 3.5). Along with the estimated outcome, there is also an estimate of the uncertainty band around the estimate which is the zone in which realistically the actual outcome may fall (see Figure 3.6).

The regression line extends beyond the range of data to forecast (X may be a time dimension).

In a perfect model, the zone of uncertainty reduces to zero and the estimated outcome is indeed the actual outcome. However, with realistic models the zone of uncertainty is nowhere close to zero (Figure 3.6). Better models have narrower bands of uncertainty compared to no-so-good-models. But the question that begs an answer (again), what is a good model?

Figure 3.5   A Forecasting Model using Regression

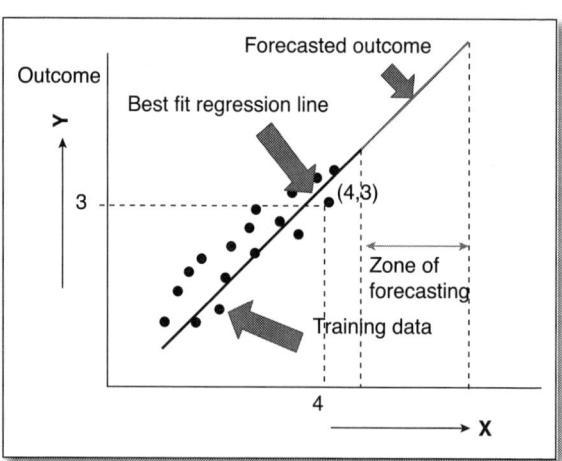

Figure 3.6   The 'Band' of Error in Forecasts

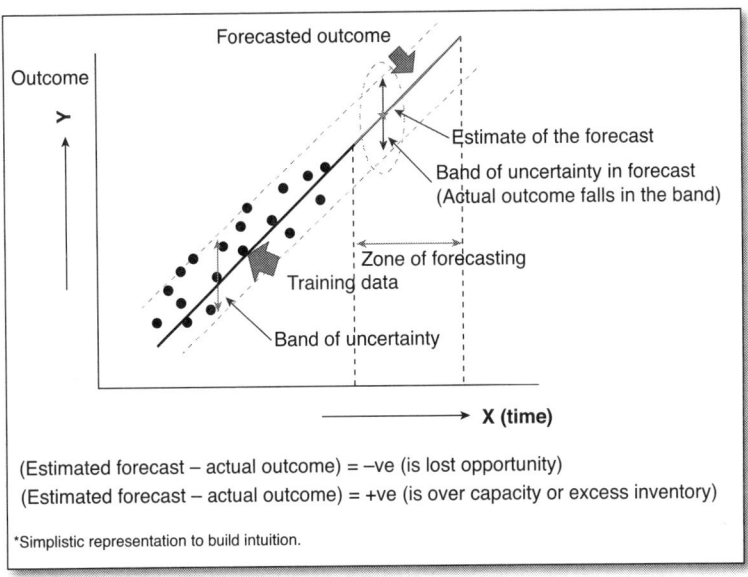

(Estimated forecast – actual outcome) = –ve (is lost opportunity)

(Estimated forecast – actual outcome) = +ve (is over capacity or excess inventory)

*Simplistic representation to build intuition.

Let us pay attention to the band of uncertainty around the estimate (Figure 3.6). If the band is wide, both the lower and the upper limit are a concern since this is the range over which the actual outcome may fall, and wider is the range, lesser is the confidence of the business planner to provide a concrete 'view' of the future outcome. For instance, if the plan is made conservative based on this model output (on the lower end of the range from the estimate) there is a higher probability of falling short of actual and vice versa. What then is a 'manageable' band of uncertainty (to be expected from a model) if a precise forecast is not available?

Model Output and Its Usability: General Insights

The generic answer to the previous question is dependent upon a few dimensions:

1. How much risk is the decision maker going to bear? Which risk is bearable and which is not?
2. How flexible are operations process to address changes in final outcome from the planned?

The risk appetite of a decision maker has a significant influence on the way the model results are interpreted. If the business loss due to 'lost opportunity' is lower than the cost of excess inventory caused due to 'optimistic planning', the planned output will be usually calibrated to a level lower than the estimate to mitigate losses due to over production/ capacity. Also, the positive deviations from planned amount (lost opportunity) can be better tolerated than negative deviations (excess production). Hence, the mandate for the analytics person would be to minimize the error band on the lower side to the extent possible. The focus of planning is reversed if the cost of 'lost opportunity' is much higher than the cost of excess inventory. In this case the error band on the positive range from the estimate requires better calibration (minimized as much as possible).

If a corrective reaction to the actual 'deviation from plan' is possible (the ability to calibrate action in real time when the future unravels and the actual outcome is known), planners would be more than comfortable with error bands in forecast that are in sync with this margin of operational flexibility. Therefore, so long as the 'quality' of the model output (error range of the forecast) matches with the range of calibration of the operations process, the estimate obtained will be deemed good for decision making.

For example, if the error band around the forecast is about ± 20 percent and the flexibility in changing plan to meet actual output is about the same, then the estimated forecast is a good input to the planning process. The intuition here is that irrespective of what the actual outcome is (within the range) actual delivery operations can seamlessly recalibrate without any significant incremental cost. Hence, if the forecast error is within this limit of flexibility, using the estimated forecast is a good planning input.

However, if the flexibility to recalibrate production/delivery is just about ± 10 percent, there is a possibility that the adjustment needed from plan may be much higher than what can be realistically achieved, both in case of a positive and a negative deviation. Here, the planner may want to decide which actual 'unmet' deviation may cost her (him) more and accordingly readjust the plan in a way to reduce the cost.

> A demand planner in steel rolling mill estimated the demand for cold roll (CR) steel every quarter. His estimate for the next quarter's sale was 238 metric tonnes (MT) with a variation of (±) 50MT. The CR steel business head accepted the forecast given that his production team had the flexibility to adjust the production volume by (±) 40MT over the quarter to calibrate with the demand. The additional variance beyond the manufacturing plant's ability to recalibrate was reasonable risk that the business head felt could be managed.

So Are We Ready to Build Models with an Objective to Help Business Decision Making?

Once the desired output of the model is well defined in terms of (a) maximum tolerable error band in case of output estimation or (b) maximum tolerable mis-classified proportion in our target category in case of a classification problem, the mandate for model development becomes relatively simple. Analysts may now seek any methodology, simple or sophisticated, so long as they are able to achieve the objective criterion of a suitable output that adds value to decision making (see Figure 3.7).

A word of caution on the methods used to develop models. More sophisticated methods, for both types of outcome variables—continuous or classification (neural

Figure 3.7 Mandate for Model Development

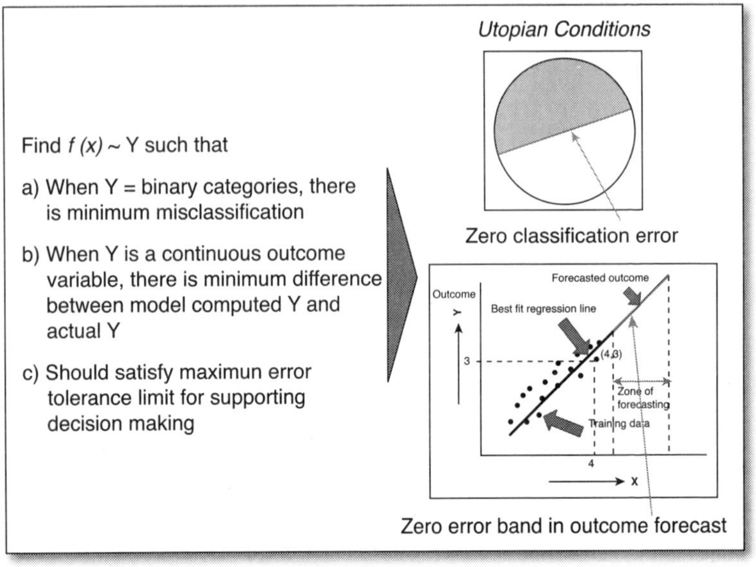
Find *f (x)* ~ Y such that
a) When Y = binary categories, there is minimum misclassification
b) When Y is a continuous outcome variable, there is minimum difference between model computed Y and actual Y
c) Should satisfy maximun error tolerance limit for supporting decision making
Utopian Conditions
Zero classification error
Forecasted outcome
Outcome
Y
Best fit regression line
3
(4,3)
Zone of forecasting
Training data
4
X
Zero error band in outcome forecast

networks, decision trees, regression splines, support vector machines)—provide an opportunity to fit the training data better and hence the performance of the models is superior (same or better than simple models). However, what is unclear is whether a better fit in the training samples amounts to reliable outcomes in other sample data (which is the true test of the usability of the model). Simple models (ordinary regression, logistic regression, contingency tables) on the other hand, may not perform as well as sophisticated models in fitting responses in the training sample, but may at times perform better than sophisticated models in other data sets.

There are automated processes for selecting models (simple or sophisticated) that best fit both training and other data (validation sample). In the process of rote search, analysts may be able to provide the best solution in a given context and compare it with the quality of outcome desired by decision makers.

With no intention to complicate matters beyond necessary, it is important to point out that actual forecasting processes in organizations require factoring in deviations beyond what the historical data used for prediction is able to identify. If the future scenario is significantly different from the past, the prediction model is not capable of factoring this pertinent deviation since no information about such scenario is available from the past data. In circumstances such as this, no data-driven model output alone will provide the right basis for choosing planning estimate. Information from outside the realm of data and modelling is required to adjust the estimate appropriately. Suffice to say, there are many other manuscripts that have addressed this matter in detail.

What have We Achieved So Far?

We have covered the generic requirement of predictive models for many marketing/business decision making. We have discussed how the quality of the model output can be ascertained in the context of a specific decision-making situation. More importantly, we have separated the exercise of setting objectives of developing predictive models from the actual process of building them. This element distinguishes the current discussion from many standard description of Predictive Analytics found in many other treatise.

In the process, we have identified a distinction between the technical function of building models using data science methods from the evaluation of the model performance on business support parameters. Decision makers and sponsors of analytics process may now have a practical approach to set realistic benchmarks for model performance without understanding the mechanics of building models.

Effective Interfacing: Be a Good Translator

For successful implementation of analytics, the technical elements of Analytics have to blend well with the business issues. We have identified a common thread around approaches, tools, techniques, metrics and business motivations that bind them all together in an effective manner in a typical organization. There has to be at least some business analytics professionals in the organization that can act as good translators. They re-jig user expectations into analytic output requirement.

Once the benchmark to evaluate business impact of the analytical output is set, it makes sense to identify the infrastructural (tool box) requirements to achieve the target.

In the next chapter, we will deal with the critical aspect of communicating analytics output in interesting ways to the end user. This is the other interface between technology and business that is critical to manage for the positive impact of Analytics (re-jigging analytic output into potential business implications).

Unfortunately, most discussions on analytics capability development initiatives stop short of this point. They rarely deal with the important issue of communicating the 'so what'. This is also a probable reason for the 'divide' between the producers and users of analytics. Telling meaningful stories using analytical output is crucial to ensure returns from this process. We shall deal with how to do this next.

4

Communicating Analytical Output:
Numbers to Narratives

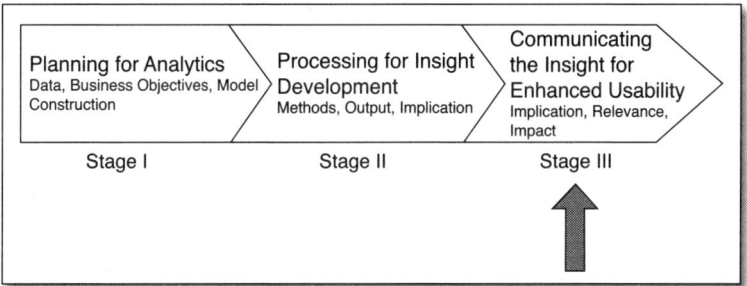

*R*avi Raj, a data analyst employed with a large sized *FMCG company was tasked to run a regression-based model on the sales volume of the company's biggest brand. He was asked to identify the important drivers of sales and report the same to Ashwin, the marketing manager.*

Ravi ran the regression on sales data and presented the output of the regression model to Ashwin, identifying the statistically significant variables that drive sales volume of the brand.

Ashwin was somewhat puzzled looking at the report. He was expecting a measure of the influence of each important

*marketing variable on the sales in terms of 'rupee impact',
so that he could get a 'business' view of the analysis. Ravi
had not expected such a push back from one of his important
internal clients, nor had he thought about how to convert his
statistically significant result into business impact. Clearly,
there was a communication gap between the two important
functional managers in the organization.*

We have reached the last and crucial stage (Stage III)
of the Analytics Process (see inset). Crucial, because the
impact of the organization's Analytics capability is usually
highly dependent on how 'well' the output is communicated
to the users. The measure of 'goodness' of the communication is based on the user group's assessment of the
relevance of the analytic input to their decision making.

Unfortunately, this is the point where many analytic
ventures falter and are less than optimally equipped to
address the concerns of business. The conversion of numeric
output into narratives (storytelling), and sometimes illustrations is important and less talked about until recently, in the
analytics domain. This chapter will provide some guidelines
about how analysts may want to structure their final output
(logically) to make better impact among their consumer
group.

We begin with some pointers on effective communication
approaches that are well established and practiced in the
knowledge industry. These are rules that are often described
in various books on effective business communication,
nevertheless, always worth a reiteration.

Building Effective Business Communication

If your words or images are not on point, making them dance in color
won't make them relevant.
—Edward Tufte, Professor Emeritus, Yale University

Making cogent arguments to substantiate a numeric output can go a long way in establishing credibility of the employee early in the analytics professional curve. It is therefore important to not only have sufficient fluency in the language of business communication (English is widely used in corporate India), but also to have expertise in structuring the communication in a way that sounds logically convincing.

Many business communication documents appear to have (a) too much process, (b) no business context, (c) too much analysis but little or no answers to business questions and (d) no main message or purpose of the communication. Hence, under these circumstances, communication tends to be 'purposeless', excruciatingly boring and, hard to decipher. Having spent many hours working on analysing the data, a relatively unstructured presentation-cum-communication plan can significantly upset the impact of such hard work, simply because the reader (audience) of the communication does not have the patience to decipher the core message presented in a laboriously constructed treatise (see Figure 4.1).

Unfortunately, by the time the presentation reaches the 'Outcome and Benefit' stage, audience are either too tired or confused with the details of the earlier stages to pay much

Figure 4.1 The Format of a Typical Process-driven Presentation

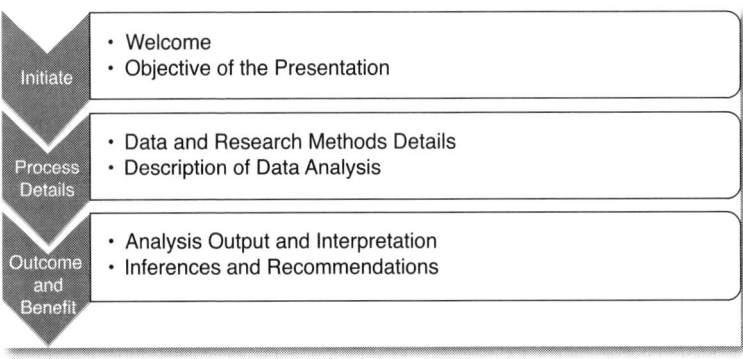

attention. For the most impactful presentation to users of analytics output, the last stage (that is, Stage III) sets the tone for the rest of the presentation. It acts as a provocation to continue with the rest of the discussion on the details of the analytics/research work, if required.

Our recommendation for many aspiring analytics professionals would be to adhere to some simple rules of structuring their communication documents to make them more impactful. We have listed some useful elements that we picked up during our professional tenure. However, we must also caution the reader to use them judiciously and only in circumstances that a logical argument needs to be provided in a business communication context.

The three main areas that a communicator needs to pay attention to[1] are:

1. The synthesis of the communication,
2. Creating a compelling structure for communication and
3. Understanding the expectation of the audience.

As stated above, the main message is the 'synthesis' of a finding (an implication or a recommendation based on the findings) rather than an exposition of facts or a summary of the same. Additionally, it should provide adequate leads into the structure of the presentation.

Creating an Impactful Structure of Presentation

A well thought out structure helps in organizing the details of the presentation effectively around the main message, so that the supporting arguments complement the veracity of the main message rather than create confusion. Practitioners

---

[1] A good reference for this material is: Barbara Minto, *The Pyramid Principle: Logic in Writing and Thinking* (London: Pitman Publishing, 1987).

have usually adopted two ways of creating effective logical structure of the presentation:

1. Top-down Hierarchical Structure
2. Sequential and Logical Organization

TOP-DOWN HIERARCHICAL STRUCTURE

In structuring the presentation in the top-down order, the main message is supported in such a manner that the evidence appears in the consequent hierarchical (lower) level. Usually the document layout begins with a page that answers the primary question (main message). Each subsequent layer in the pyramid is used to provide supporting evidence to the message in the layer above. Usually, up to five supporting points are used to optimally create an effective message (Figure 4.2).

This presentation format ensures a defensible argument for all assertions made in an anticipated hierarchical manner.

Figure 4.2   Pyramid Structure for Presenting Supporting Arguments

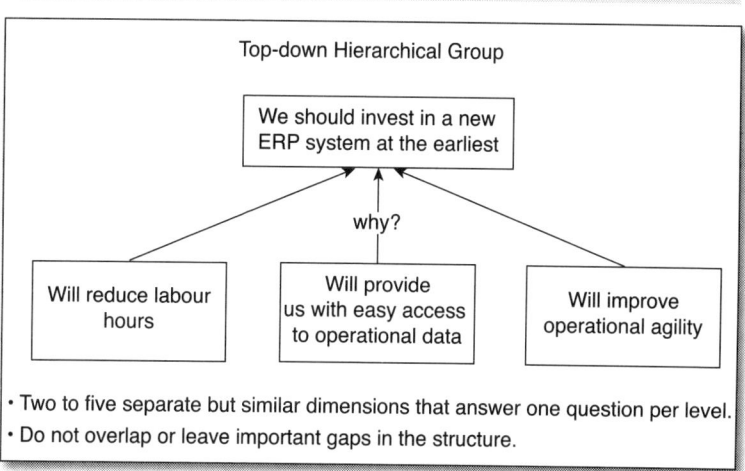

Top-down Hierarchical Group

We should invest in a new ERP system at the earliest

why?

Will reduce labour hours

Will provide us with easy access to operational data

Will improve operational agility

• Two to five separate but similar dimensions that answer one question per level.
• Do not overlap or leave important gaps in the structure.

The value of the hierarchy is that it enables the audience (reader) to sequentially move from the essence of the document to the details and allows a premature closure of the presentation without compromising on comprehensiveness, should the reader feel that (s)he does not require further factual support beyond a certain level of detail.

SEQUENTIAL AND LOGICAL ORGANIZATION

This format (Figure 4.3) is useful when an argument can be posed in a logical sequence beginning with the description of the context which provides a firm background to the presented problem that requires a business resolution. The main message is usually an emphatic reinforcement of the resolution. It is necessary to ensure a logical flow

Figure 4.3 Sequenced Logical Structure of Presenting Supporting Arguments

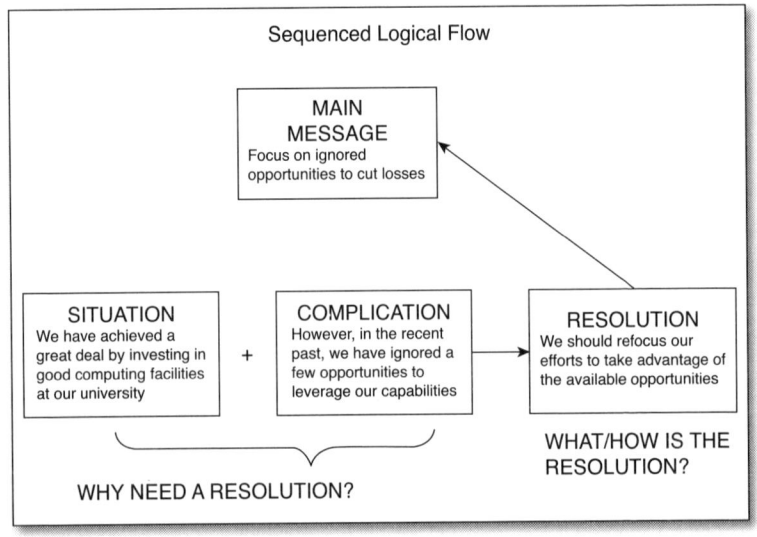

between the three parts of the argument, that is, Situation, Complication and the Resolution. Specifically, the description of the context (Situation) should provide logical cues for the problem definition (Complication) and the latter should be so presented that arguably there can be only one Resolution option, which is the one presented. In this way, the document ensures that the reader is provided with a convincing solution to the business problem being addressed.

Managing the Audience's Expectations

This should not be hard to comprehend. While we are not suggesting the presenters should 'play to the gallery', it is essential to try to get a prior notion regarding the motivations of the audience, what they might be 'looking for' and how might one 'arrest their attention'. This endeavour may also include ascertaining the appropriate means of communication and the frequency at which it should be made. Simple but significant details regarding the communication format can go a long way in ensuring the correct impact for the desired outcome.

It is necessary to remember always that the audience cares to listen to what it wants to hear, not what the presenter wants to say. If it does not hear content in line what it wants to hear, it may lead to boredom and disengagement and ultimately a perceived lack of impact. On the other hand, if it hears something contradictory to its expectation, it may provoke a dispute, leading to an involved discussion on the research methodology. This situation serves the purpose of conducting the research and brings out useful insights and 'surprises'. Analysts must be prepared for situations where disputes arise (a sign of involvement of the audience), since they are the opportunities to prove the real worth of analytics and research.

Telling Stories Through Data

We end this section of the book on the theme that was offered in Introduction. The role of the analysts is to 'tell useful stories, only that they are backed by data'. The art of storytelling is a strange concoction of (a) understanding data insights and interpreting their impact, (b) converting them into creative language, yet focused with an objective to make a point and (c) building visual imagery (where possible) to drive the impact (see Figure 4.4). In the process, the analyst ensures the consumer's total engagement of her research to the main points that she would like to drive home. That is more than a handful of skills to build for a person in this profession, not necessarily something that can be acquired overnight.

Mere reporting of facts based on a technical process is clichéd and no longer valued as useful in the practicing world. Hence, creative capabilities (although incongruous with traditional analytical capabilities) have to be encouraged in organizations to ensure effective portrayal of information output.

Figure 4.4 How to Sell Analytic Insights?

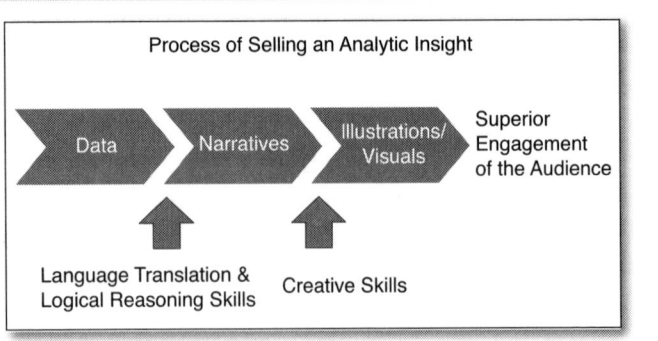

How Could Ravi Raj Have Done a Better Job of Communicating Results?

To illustrate the above point with an example, we go back to Ravi Raj's problem of convincing Ashwin about the value of his analysis (see vignette at the beginning of the chapter). If, instead of showcasing the regression output (driver coefficients with statistical significance) which very few practitioners without statistical training appreciate, Ravi had managed to depict the impact of the coefficients of various marketing variables in terms of the volume sales as depicted in the illustration (Figure 4.5), Ashwin would perhaps have been more convinced.

The data (regression coefficients) had to be converted into an accounting metric which depicted 'sales volume attributable' to a particular marketing variable. When all such metric were added, together they accounted for the

Figure 4.5   Marketing Mix Model Output Presentation

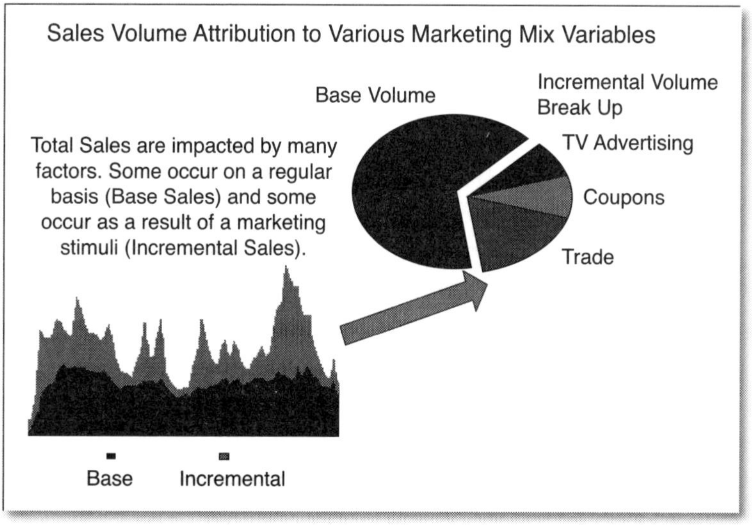

total sales volume of the brand. In Figure 4.5, for instance, the incremental volume is explained by volume driven by (a) TV Advertising, (b) Coupons and, (c) Trade. In turn, the total of the 'Incremental' volume (made up by these three components) and the 'Base' volume, made up for the Volume Sales of the brand. This is a practical way of accounting for volume sales and making various marketing variables 'accountable' for the same.[2]

It is necessary to emphasize that creative communication is not always compatible with technical rigour (something analytics is known for). However, 'measured' approximations to increase usefulness of the information, at the cost of precision is something worth striving for. Admittedly, this requires the power of appropriate calibration that is achieved only with experience and a superior understanding of the underlying analytics process. Hence, business leaders may well be advised to invest in this very critical capability as early as possible to ensure a fruitful organizational culture of creative use of information over time.

What Next?

In the next chapter, we would like to share our views on scaling up analytics capability in organizations which necessarily means building infrastructure and technology-based automation (of some form). Many organizations tend to invest in such infrastructure since they lend a material change in the 'capability' of the organization. So far, we have discussed building healthy analytics culture within

---

[2] Readers may refer to Gene Zelazny, *Say it with Charts: The Executive's Guide to Visual Communication* (IL, USA: Irwin, 1996) for more details on Visual Communication.

organization by keeping the 'line of sight' on the business objectives. Whether building infrastructure should, (a) precede culture (the cause for cultural change), (b) develop simultaneously or (c) be an investment that satiates a 'hunger' developed due to a healthy analytics culture in the organization, is still a matter of heated debate.

5

From Analysis to Analytics: Building the Infrastructure

*R*ohan Bajpai has been newly appointed as the Chief Digital Officer of a large consumer durable marketing company. He has been tasked with building a comprehensive digital plan for the organization which would include managing its digital data repository, leveraging the data using effective business analytic platforms and also facilitating many of the company operations seamlessly on the digital interface. Rohan's challenge is to ensure this upscaling of the organization's infrastructure happens without any major disruptions in the productivity of the organization.

Surely, this would require him to understand the organization and its operating environment very well, before suggesting any changes to the infrastructure and the operating protocol. Any investment would require both a thorough assessment of its returns and its criticality. Finally, he will perhaps have to deal with the eternal question: why do we need this change, especially when the business is doing fine?

The question often crosses a business leader's mind: How do we define the point where there is a transition from analysis to analytics? Does that point clearly exist or is it still fuzzy and many a times stated by the organization's nomenclature? Earlier in the book we have defined 'Analytics' as the process of analysis of data that is done logically, aided by the sciences (statistical, computers, etc.).

We share the following experience:

A couple of weeks ago, two Masters students (MBA) who have graduated last academic year walked into my faculty office. Amongst many things, we talked about their job profile. They both work for 2 IT majors in India in the respective 'Analytics' team as Analysts. Curiosity led me to ask them the nature of Analytics done by their teams. One of the students said that her team is involved in assimilating data from various data sources of the organization for relationship and pattern analysis. Most of the data is structured and categorical in nature, hence statistical software for categorical data analysis is used. The second student said that his team is involved in rollout of a technology solution for a client in a developed nation. The data is mostly unstructured in nature whereby feasibility tests have to be conducted against the requirements specified by the client. This involves using statistical software package for predictive analysis'.

This somewhere corroborates the hypothesis that analysis done based on facts is called Analytics in organizations in India, the degree of analysis may vary across organizations.

There has been a gradual transition from analysis to analytics, from identifying simple insights from data to complex pattern analysis and prediction methodologies, an indication towards use of sophisticated business intelligence solutions. Competitive environment and sustainability efforts by business enterprises have introduced business intelligence as an agenda item in boardroom discussion. It is an important part of strategic level discussions where the focus is on the degree of need of business intelligence solutions within the organization and its benefits. However the question is, who addresses such queries, is it the CIO or the Data Scientist, the functional team heads, the technology heads in the company, the vendors who have been associated with the company for a long time for providing enterprise technology solutions or the newly hired executive in the role of Big Data Solutions Architect?

How does the individual who addresses such issues, say Rohan, prepare himself for the discussion? A simple question, as it may appear, asked to him by a board member, 'Does our organization need to upgrade from existing Enterprise solution to new Business Analytics solution?' has multiple parameters that need to be accounted for before responding confidently to the query. Figure 5.1 describes the four aspects that need to be considered before preparing the slides of a power point presentation by Rohan for the boardroom discussion.

Figure 5.1   Steps to Identify Need for New BI Solution

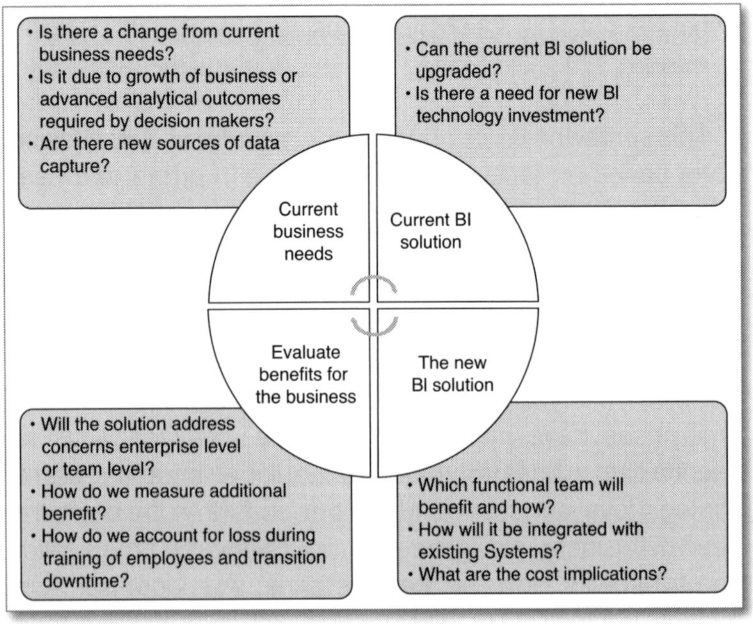

1. CURRENT BUSINESS NEEDS

This refers to re-visiting the business objectives of the organization and identifying any changing needs. In order to do this, Rohan has to be very thorough with the business dynamics of the organization. This does not happen overnight, and hence usually he and his team will conduct in-depth interviews with functional heads of the organization and focus group discussions with various team members over a period of time. Rohan will have in his team a mix of business leaders from within the organization who will primarily provide the bridge between the business and the technology groups, data analysts, members from information technology team, statisticians and a couple of members from the vendor organization that has proposed the alternate BI solution. The questions of interest to Rohan would be to understand the degree of utilization of the existing BI solution by the business leaders for decision making. However, Rohan will not talk about the technology piece at all during his conversation with the business teams. It is observed that whenever there is a discussion about a business intelligence solution, off the end user goes talking about the required software and hardware challenges, followed by integrating it with company data and processes. However, Rohan and his team know that is not what is required from the conversation. Hence, Rohan will have to steer the conversation to understand the kind of decision making that is necessary by the respective business teams and to what degree the analytics tool facilitates data interpretation, manipulation and inferences by the end users. He needs to further possess the business acumen to be able to understand how data is interpreted by the respective teams and where are the gaps which can be addressed to aid better interpretation for decision making. Quite a challenge isn't it? Where do we get a resource person like Rohan? Are the educational institutions in India doing enough to create resources like Rohan who can be absorbed for jobs that are flooding the market? Business schools in India are including courses on Business Analytics and Data Mining to train students to be industry-ready, however it is still at a very nascent stage.

2. CURRENT BI SOLUTION

It is important for Rohan and his team to evaluate the existing BI solution from its technical standpoint. Rohan will try to compare the inputs received from business heads (point 1) and map it to business analytics features of the existing BI solution. Analytics has very different meaning for different business leaders: it could range from a frequency analysis of categorical data to a 3D graphical predictive analysis tool. Many organizations use optimization model for monitoring and calibration purposes. New technology solutions for business analytics by big technology companies have flooded the market in the past few years. They have provided solutions for Descriptive, Predictive and Prescriptive Analytics. Solutions have also emphasized the significance of integrating information from varied information sources for rich and faster decision making, the need for considering the pace at which data is captured (in some cases it is real time in nature), and compartmentalize the consolidated data effectively for separate decision-making teams. These solutions have been developed to complement the existing Enterprise solutions in most big companies. These Enterprise solutions are either designed as modular solutions for respective functional teams that tie into the overall organization information system or they exist as pieces of solutions like Customer Relationship Management (CRM), Supply

Chain Management (SCM) or Knowledge Management (KM) systems. The KM systems have subsequently been able to create organizational level centralized knowledge base that allows sharing of knowledge and best practices across global locations. These platforms have also facilitated basic level analysis of information, as required by managers, for decision making. The software packages and solutions in the market are very tempting as they promise advanced analytics and premium outcomes. The end user is lured without complete clarity of the end result. The challenge for Rohan and his team would be as follows: to evaluate whether, for fulfilling the changing business needs put forth from point 1, there is a need for purchase of new BI solution or would an upgrade to the existing solution suffice. Points like cost implications, return on investment, technology compatibility and data security, all rest on the shoulders of Rohan and his team.

3. THE NEW BI SOLUTION

Rohan and his team have been able to summarize from the findings in points 1 and 2 that a new BI solution with advanced business analytics capability will address the requirements of the end users. Rohan's next task would be to evaluate the new BI solution in terms of its compatibility with the existing technology infrastructure within the organization. Organization structure may be of different types: it could be a large organization with centralized resources at one location (family business firms), or an organization in India with offices in several locations (a bank or a manufacturing company), or a brick and mortar company that has online presence too, or a completely online company. Rohan, based on his understanding of his company's business will evaluate integration of the new BI solution with the old in terms of technology upgrade, data capture (ETL–extraction, transformation, loading) methods, new sources and types of data, storage and information security concerns, sharing of information across teams and the costs involved.

4. EVALUATE BENEFITS FOR THE BUSINESS

If Rohan and his team are able to present a convincing case in the boardroom that receives a go ahead; he will need to plan its implementation. In large organizations, the practice is to perform a pilot test with a group of prospective users. Any immediate implementation and user interface issues can be taken care of at this point. After successfully conducting the pilot test, it is implemented to the larger user group. The implementation is usually done in a phased manner, meaning piece by piece. After users become comfortable with the first phase rollout, the next phase is considered. This creates minimal downtime in business, manages the training of employees and ensures a smooth transition. However, Rohan pauses for a minute and wonders, is it all that easy? No, any technology upgrade comes with teething problems. The magic lies in how well it is planned for a smooth transition. So the question goes back to whether it is technology first or data analytics first? Here we are considering data analytics as the need for managers to make faster decisions aided by judicious data interpretation based on facts. Rohan is a firm believer that the following viewpoint, although theoretically it may seem easy but practically can never be possible: the firm should invest in a technology solution first, and then think of what additional benefits it may provide for better decision making. He picks up a paper and pencil and jots down the questions that he needs to prepare to answer the management: Is the investment necessary? What is it that we are not doing now that gets solved by the technology solution? What business analytics decisions are we thinking about doing differently? How much of customization is involved and does the vendor promise the customization from the canned solution? Who champions it internally within the organization, is the team of champions experienced enough to understand the business needs and convert the requirements during the rollout? Has the required feasibility analysis for breakeven on costs incurred in purchasing the technology solution and meeting up to the competitors done, and what do the numbers say? Who provides the training for the new technology and does it actually aid better decision making?

Emerging Technologies That Aid Business Analytics

The cyclic process of technology companies coming up with new ways to capture data and process them into information, leading to organizations adopting the technology solutions and thus consciously or unconsciously build a huge repository of data, has continued over the years. With so many different choices talking of benefits to business in different forms, the organizations are treading carefully. More so because it is not just about the technology solution, but meeting the challenge of all pieces of the adoption of technology needs to fall in line together for the desired outcome. Some decisions to purchase new technology solutions come from end users who are practitioners and know that a particular analytics tool will facilitate better decision making. In such cases, the particular group of users are provided with technology upgrade/purchase for the specific needs ensuring that it ties into the overall firm architecture. In other cases, technology solutions (software or hardware) are purchased at enterprise level which affects a large group of

Figure 5.2   Emerging Technologies Facilitate Advanced Analytics

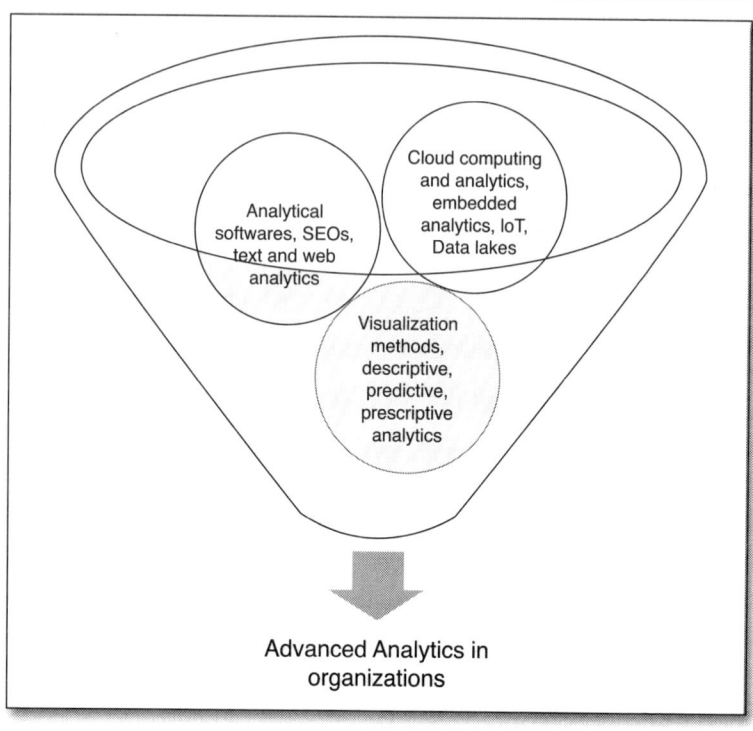

users. Figure 5.2 lists some of the technologies that have led to our discussion on business analytics (we offer them in the increasing order of complexity):

VISUALIZATION METHODS

With the advancement of technology, Dashboards have become popular in organizations as visualization methods. From simple analysis to displaying complex metrics, there has been a slow and steady transition across the industry value chain. What it essentially does is, summarizing the information available from various sources and presenting it in a user friendly form. In principal, similar to the concept of Exploratory Analysis that was discussed in Chapter 2.

Decision makers have appreciated the dashboards as it allows collecting, analysing and presenting huge amount of data being captured by organizations daily and additionally the real time availability of the information. Drill down techniques allows diving into further details of a specific result displayed on the screen. Consolidated data can be represented in forms of charts, tables and other desirable representation methods for senior management to make decisions by considering many aspects of the business simultaneously.

Dashboards fall in the category of embedded analytics. According to Gartner analyst Kurt Schlegel, traditional business intelligence was suffering in 2008 due to a lack of integration between the data and the business users. Embedded analytics allows embedding business intelligence into operational applications and business processes thus

Real Analytics: The Retail Dashboard

There is sample data, loads and loads of it, in varied forms. Data on varied brands, sales information, buyer details, region-wise performance data and trend across the years. The top management is interested in having a birds-eye view of overall firm performance by looking at all the metrics at a glance and a need to drill down the data for specific details. Additionally, the marketing team requires information for profiling the customers, monitoring sales, identifying the large and small selling products, region-wise differences in costs-versus-sales volume, identifying the leads and so on. Does the CEO or the marketing executive think technology while making the decisions? No, it is the information available on hand and then the associated gut feel from the years of work experience in the industry. However they do know that company performance metrics can now be monitored in much more detail due to the availability of advanced methods of data capture and technology tools. The visualization platforms known commonly as Retail dashboards are used in organizations to monitor firm performance and aid decision making.

allowing users to be able to make relevant interpretations from consolidated information.

Real Analytics: Bubble Charts

Bubble charts are simple visualization tool, an excellent way of showing data by bubbles in 2 dimensional graphs. It looks at historical data and from Identified indicators, compares them over a period of time. A leading retail chain has presence in several cities in India. It also has an online presence. The merchandise is distributed across various locations of the store based on sales data. It uses bubble charts for monitoring region-wise sales.

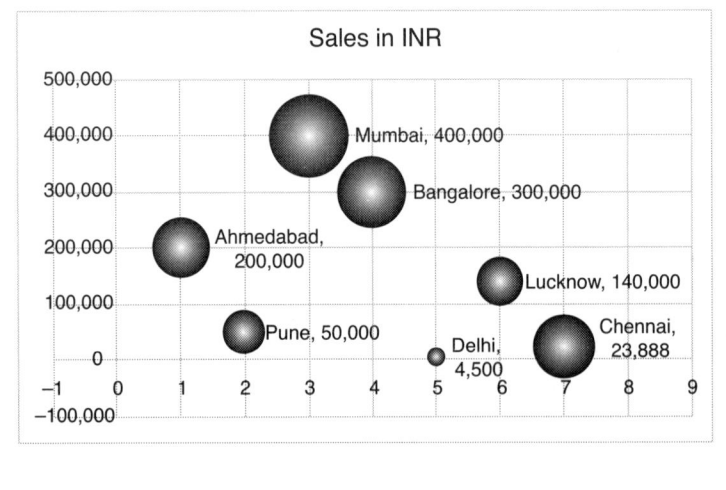

CLOUD COMPUTING

The advent of Cloud computing came as a refreshing relief to businesses across the globe. Cloud computing (Source: Wikipedia) is a type of Internet-based *computing* that provides shared *computer*-processing resources and data to computers and other devices on demand. It allows sharing of resources across various locations from servers hosted on the internet. This has direct implication on saving costs as it implies maintaining less local infrastructure with the additional benefit of exchanging and sharing information across virtual teams. The three basic methodologies that are prevalent for cloud computing are Infrastructure as a Service (IaaS) wherein the organization utilizes storage capacity space on a provider's infrastructure, Platform as a Service (PaaS) wherein the development tools for application development is on the provider's infrastructure and the third is Software as a Service (SaaS) wherein the provider offers web services like email over the internet in a distributed model. It offers the flexibility of paying for computer resources on a pay per use basis or on-demand use. Cloud computing can be private (data within the organization premises, controlled and distributed by a centralized server), public (hosted on a provider's server) or a mix of both called hybrid service which allows maintaining privacy of confidential company data yet outsources the mundane bulky routine data-processing

---

Real Analytics: Cloud Computing in Airlines

Cloud computing has provided immense cost benefits and flexibility in the service industry with the benefit of scalability. Airlines have adopted this technology to manage huge volume of customer and operational data processing. IaaS has reduced the requirement of maintaining large technology infrastructure within the organization. Additionally, real time data can be pulled in from various sources and analysed for better service to customers as well as internal operational decisions. The customer touch points like airline staff, security personnel, visa check points have information on customers check-in, luggage, destination, meal plans, loyalty cards and other specific details. Thus the entire reservation system is managed on the cloud. Operational decisions—on aircraft maintenance, routes, weather and complaint handling—can be made using data on the cloud. This allows internal decision makers to focus on strategic level issues rather than day-to-day operations.

tasks. The logic is very simple and understood by top management of organizations for implementing cloud strategy. Since 2009, many companies have begun going the cloud computing way for faster decision making.

INTERNET OF THINGS (IOT)

With advent of time, the top management was told about Cloud Analytics with IoT (Internet of Things) Gateways. That sure becomes confusing. Analytics itself means an advanced form of statistics for a common man. The top management executive starts to wonder that the company is doing well with analysis using cloud computing what is the need for Cloud Analytics with IoT Gateways? What ain't broke, why fix it? On the other side, the technology executives have a convincing story on the benefits of this emerging technology. Collecting information from varied sensor devices is the need of the hour to be able to track and understand data being generated simultaneously from varied sources. Wikipedia defines Internet of Things (IoT) as the inter-networking of physical devices, vehicles, buildings and other items embedded with electronics, software, sensors, actuators and network connectivity that enables these objects to collect and exchange data.

The advantage of IoT allows objects to be sensed and/or controlled over existing network infrastructure. This results in better efficiency, accuracy and cost benefits for the organiza-tion. Usually this requires a phased upgrade to existing tech-nology infrastructure, which the business leader conducts a meeting with Rohan and his team and then decides on further investment in technology.

DATA LAKES

We have talked about Data repositories in Chapter 3. Data warehouses have well designed repository wherein

Real Analytics: Smart Electricity Grids

Government of India initiative of Smart City includes creating a smart electricity infrastructure backbone across India: The Smart Grid. This plans to provide smart metering facility at customers' residence, automation in distribution of electricity, manage electricity load and usage in real-time, identify any problems in the grid operations using sensors providing status update, flexible electricity pricing by demand side management processes, capturing electricity from renewable sources like solar rooftops at consumer locations et al. The utility providers have started working on significant changes for integration into the central smart grid like upgrading technology infrastructure, addition of a digital method of communication and streamlining existing processes. In smart grid, data will be collected from various sensor points located within the grid infrastructure or at consumer location and real time analytics will provide dependable electricity to larger masses at lower cost, lower downtimes, less transmission and distribution losses, faster response to complaints.

data resides in a structured form. Analytical processes are carried out by business leaders using software packages. For specific functional team, at times, Data marts are created to serve specific business needs. The data marts, which are a subset of the data warehouse, allow access rights for specific user groups and speed up the process of query, data transfer and analysis at individual department level. Business leaders have been asking Rohan and his team about data lakes in recent times. Data lakes are similar to data warehouses as both are used to store data. However, data lakes store data in raw form in large scale as it is captured from the source unlike data warehouse where it is stored methodically to facilitate analytical processes. In many organizations, business leaders are using a hybrid solution for their analytical needs. The raw data whether unstructured data, text, audio, video, web data, sensor data are all stored together in a data lake. It can compartmentalize the data depending on the source from where it is received or the requirement of the business teams. Simple analysis on this data can provide insights that may be of interest to the business teams. This analysis' result can be fed to the enterprise data warehouse where further analytical tests can be carried out.

ANALYTICAL SOFTWARE PACKAGES

Business leaders who have made decisions based on outcomes of statistical analysis have been passionate about the features of the analytical software being used. They do not necessarily need to understand the coding, however the features of the package help them articulate their business needs into possible inputs to the analytical software. Rohan and his team will always be there to facilitate, but one must remember that the analytical process outcome must be such that is useful for the business leader. Useful here means that it can be understood and interpreted by the user group,

---

Real Analytics: Data Lakes in Consumer Banking

Banking industry is striving to be agile to face stiff competition in the consumer banking space. Customers are becoming more demanding, and banks are making efforts to provide fast, quality service from across the world. Customer data in retail banking resides in enterprise data warehouse on a centralized server and is distributed across locations depending on the business team's needs. It consists of gathering data real-time from various customer touch points, be it from a bank branch location, ATMs, web banking or mobile banking. Enterprise data lakes have injected agility in providing banking services at lower costs. Data is picked from all customer touch points and processed in the data lake to be fed into the Enterprise data warehouse.

and provide further insights that aid decision making. Many new software packages are available in the market and IT companies are providing support for necessary rollout and after-sales support. We look at 3 examples where the degree of analysis using statistical software varies, yet they all fall into the definition of analytics done by the particular organizations discussed.

From the above three examples we reiterate that analytics, as it may seem popular and trending in recent times, is an age old practice in organizations. It is the culture within the organization that would allow it to change nomenclature with the changing environment, else remain with the same nomenclature and keep improving on processes as the need of the business changes.

There are other situations where data gets captured as a result of a technology tool that is being used in the organization. The business leaders are aware that such volumes of data exist, however they do not know what to do with it; keep it or junk it. There is always the inner voice that echoes there may

---

Real Analytics: Temperature Monitoring System

A global healthcare firm had purchased a temperature and humidity monitoring system from a vendor to monitor 400 sensitive items stored in the refrigeration unit at their company headquarters. The system was customised to suit the needs of the user group within the organization. It had installed sensors at critical location in the refrigeration unit from where it would capture information and generate log at regular intervals. In case of any irregularity, it would generate a beep with an LED light indicator for required action. It would also suggest possible corrective actions. Every month-end it would provide a report of abnormalities during the month and corrective measures taken. This data would also be recorded in the enterprise data warehouse. This falls in the category of basic Analytics.

Real Analytics: Natural Gas Pipeline

A natural gas processing and distribution company in India uses business analytics while planning for pipeline laying in India. It has built a network of trunk pipelines covering the length of India. It plays a key role as gas market developer in India for decades, catering to major industrial sectors like power, fertilizers and city gas distribution. While laying new pipes, it is done such that it is close to demand centres (customer locations). This has direct cost implication on the day-to-day service, resulting in huge cost savings. Route mapping (path to follow) for new pipelines and capacity considerations work with multivariate scenarios using statistical software to determine minimum length between points. Laying is normally straight unless there are impediments like a forest area, which have to be avoided due to environmental concerns. Pipeline laying is expensive and hence proper diagnosis and planning needs to be done by the roll-out teams so that there are no surprises after a work has been initiated. The degree of Analytics involved is of higher order compared to the previous example of healthcare firm. However, within the organization, still no 'Analytics' team exists. It is based on analysis being carried out at the functional team level.

Real Analytics: Taxi Service Dynamic Pricing Model

A taxi service company works in a marketplace model. It does not own the taxis but works with transportation providers who provide taxi service. They have to depend on, the drivers being available at the time when the customer requires a taxi, and at the point of location where it is needed. The taxi service company works on a low-price model, where they charge lower than their competitors. However, there are times when traffic may be higher due to weekends or evening hours or festival dates. During such times, to ensure availability of service, the price per ride is higher. It works on an analytical predictive dynamic pricing model.

be gold residing within this data, it just needs to be unfolded. Many organizations have made efforts to understand and analyse the data for useful business insights.

Real Analytics: Petroleum Company Upstream

A petroleum company in India operates along the entire hydrocarbon value chain. During the upstream operation of oil exploration, mainly two types of data are captured.

1. Raw seismic data (aerial and ground {surface and sub-surface}) gets collected and stored.
2. Well-data (production, drilling, lab data and logs) captured at each depth.

Any new drilling activity begins with aerial survey followed by ground survey. In case of leads, the drilling test beds are created to conduct preliminary drilling to identify possibilities of finding wells. Raw data captured during these activities is pre-processed at the RCC (Regional Computer Center). Samples of seismic log data and well-data are analysed further. The seismic data are unstructured and require advanced methods to pre-process, cleanse and then store for further analysis. Well-data on the other hand are structured transactional data. Client and Project teams require information for planning and forecasting while making decision on carrying out seismic activities in new fields. Additionally, when actual well drilling activity is carried out, historical data provides useful information. Visualization of the data in the desired form is key to appropriate decision making. Visualization techniques such as digitized maps with colour coding provide depth and clarity. Certain standard queries are run to make analysed data available on a regular basis. Reports from standard queries are run to address the Project team's requirements. Use of a huge virtual reality interpretation facility allows the clients to make further decisions on carrying out seismic and drilling activities by studying the results of interpretations.

SEARCH ENGINE OPTIMIZATION (SEO)

Search Engine Optimization (SEO) has become a topic of discussion in the industry corridors since the time companies started operating online retail stores along with brick and mortar presence, followed by companies that offered buying completely online. SEO captures what customers search for; based on keywords of the site, the time spent on each page, number of visits. It also includes optimizing the site to show up higher during search results displayed by search engines like Google. Appearing in more searches means the possibility of a visit resulting into a sale of product on the website. Higher level of analytics is performed based on metrics captured from consumer search behaviour. Several online sites like stattools.com, statvoo.com, informer.com, similarityweb.com and so on, have used website usage metrics information and have analysed it using SEO tools and statistical methods.

TEXT AND WEB ANALYTICS

A huge amount of data exists in unstructured form on the internet. Websites have been created with large amount of textual content. There are opinion and discussion sites containing text in threads of continuous conversations. Blogs and personal homepages generate unstructured data. Retail sites contain unstructured information like the textual data of the website content, customer buying habits, queries and complaints, social media posts, research reports and so on. Analysts have developed ways of mining this rich source of data for developing insights that can be useful for business growth and profitability. Sentiments that are expressed by stakeholders are a rich source of information which, if analysed, can generate interesting business insights. Statistical methods like web and text analytics for evaluating web and textual content on the web sites have become important in analysing unstructured data. Sentiment analysis, also known as opinion mining, forms an important component of industry requirement where opinion expressed by individual in textual content is analysed using natural language processing for subjective responses. Opinions are identified and categorized for positive or negative sentiments expressed by the respondents.

Text mining/analytics, also known as text data mining or knowledge discovery in textual databases, is the semi-automated process of extracting patterns (useful information and knowledge) from large amount of unstructured data sources. Text mining is the same as data mining in that it has the same purpose and uses the same processes, but with text mining, the input to the process is a collection of unstructured (or less structured) data files such as Word documents, PDF files, text excerpts, XML files and so on. In essence, text mining can be thought of as a process (with two main steps) that starts with imposing structure to the text-based data sources followed by extracting relevant information and knowledge from this structured data, using data mining techniques and tools.

The World Wide Web is perhaps the world's largest data and text repository, and the amount of information on the Web is growing rapidly every day. A lot of interesting information can be found online: whose homepage is linked to which other pages, how many people have links to a specific webpage, and how a particular site is organized. In addition, each visitor to a website, each search on a search engine, each click on a link, and each transaction on an e-commerce site creates additional data. Although unstructured textual data in the form of webpages coded in HTML or XML are the dominant content of the web, the web infrastructure also contains hyperlink information (connections to other webpages) and usage information (logs of visitors interactions with websites), all of which provide rich data for knowledge discovery. Analysis of this information can help us make better use of websites and also aid us in enhancing relationships and value to the visitors of our own websites. Web mining (or web data mining)

Real Analytics: Text and Web Analytics in Online Grocery

With growing number of e-tailers providing online platform for grocery shopping, competition has entered the online grocery shopping market in India. Research and academic discussion forums debate competitive strategies for their growth and survival. Some of the common attributes of measuring online presence in a competitive market include the bouquet of product categories offered, the ability to service pan-India, competitive pricing, on-time delivery of products and services, discounts offered through deals and coupons, maintaining quality, managing suppliers, handling consumer complaints effectively and so on. While the content displayed on the website is important along with the look and feel, easy loading of pages, quick navigation between web page links, appearing in searches, referrals from other web sites and a desirable revenue model; equally important is to maintain the optimum products in the inventory, on-time delivery, cash back options, deals and discounts, payment options and handling customer queries and complaints. All of these activities generate a huge amount of data that are structured as well as unstructured in nature. Some of the data is consciously captured by the organizations which are used by their analytics teams to do descriptive and predictive analysis and devise competitive strategies and metrics for measurement of their success online.

is the process of discovering intrinsic relationships (that is, interesting and useful information) from web data, which are expressed in the form of textual, linkage, or usage information.[1]

Ending Remarks

The amount of data available to the business teams in organizations have brought a sure change in the way teams operate

---

[1]   E. Turban, R. Sharda, D. Delen, and D. King, *Business Intelligence: A Managerial Approach*, 2nd ed. (India: Pearson, 2011).

and make decisions. Spontaneous judgemental remarks by a senior member in the team based on gut feel, claiming it on years of work experience can be challenged by a new joiner based on factual evidence. Business leaders ensure that judgemental remarks are supported by information. This information may be a result of quick analysis using spread sheet software or complex statistical analysis, the significance lies in understanding the outcome of the analysis and interpreting it to address the objectives of the problem statement. This has cultivated an environment of fact-based decision making within organizations. Additionally, there are huge reserves of data on company servers. Enthusiast business leaders make attempts to look at data sitting idle on the servers, data that has been captured as a result of running certain routine business processes. Their attempt is to identify usefulness of the data by finding the gold that can be reaped from its appropriate analysis and interpretation.

Figure 5.3 Joining the Dots of Analytics

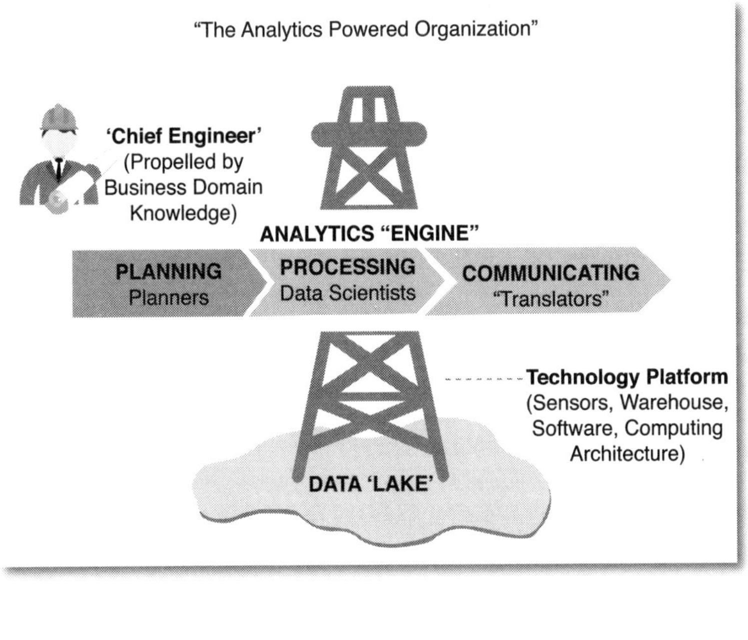

"The Analytics Powered Organization"

'Chief Engineer'
(Propelled by Business Domain Knowledge)

ANALYTICS "ENGINE"

| **PLANNING** | **PROCESSING** | **COMMUNICATING** |
| Planners | Data Scientists | "Translators" |

- - - - - **Technology Platform**
(Sensors, Warehouse, Software, Computing Architecture)

DATA 'LAKE'

We as academicians, meet industry leaders during short term training programs organized for them at our institute. They are in decision-making roles from various industry segments. In the analytics classroom discussions, there is excitement amongst them to share their role as business analytics drivers within their respective organizations. The nature of work varies from analysis of categorical data, tracking and monitoring using optimization models, descriptive and trend analysis, predictive analytics and text/web analytics. It can be concluded that there is a gradual move from analysis to analytics, yet technology surfaces the discussion very quickly. As business leaders, one must continue the focus on business needs and develop the skills to interpret outcomes from analytical-processing results, and based on such interpretations, further be able to create useful insights that aid agile decision making. Technology tools will continue to remain a platform (see Figure 5.3), appropriate use, ably calibrated by domain knowledge, will provide desired results.

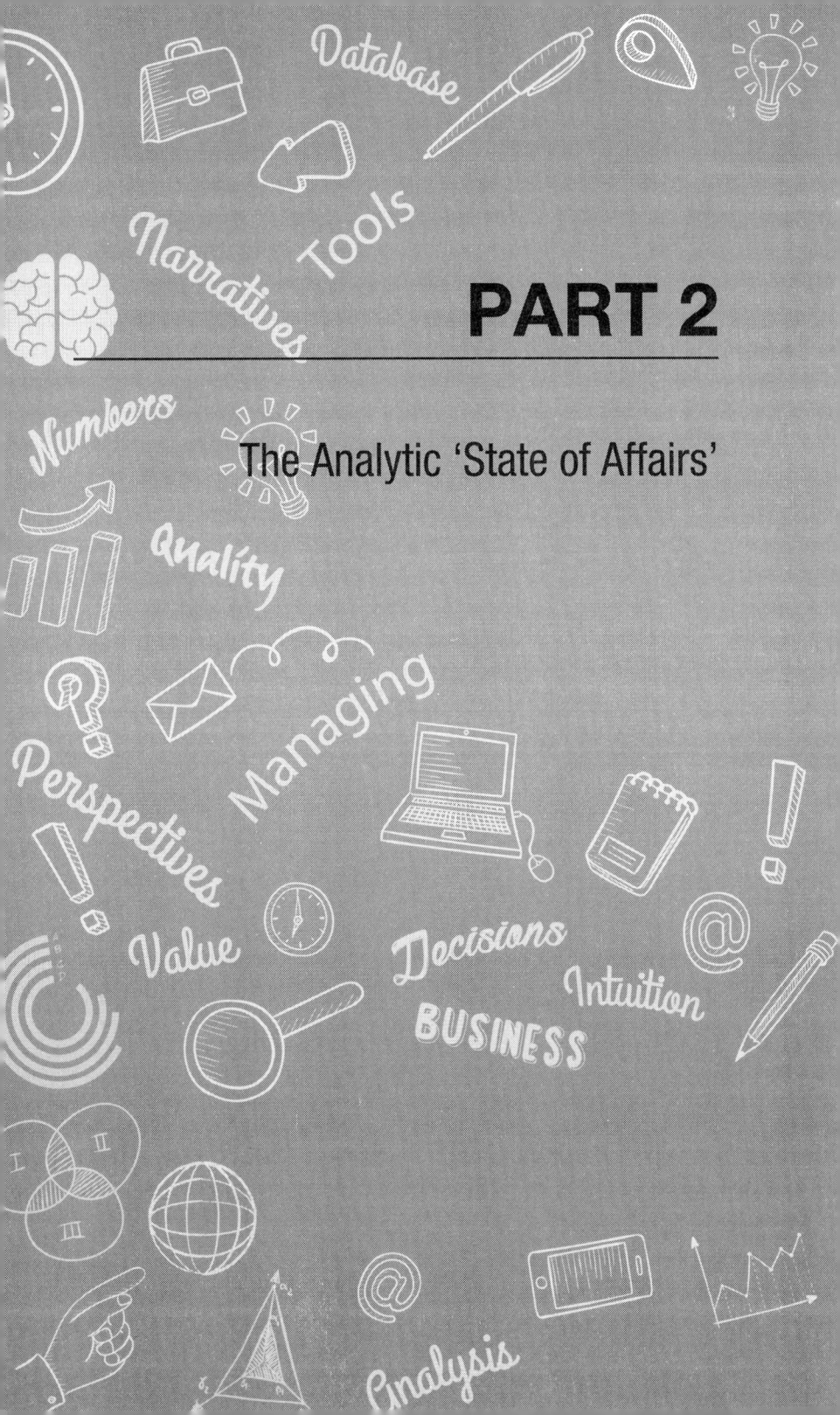

PART 2

The Analytic 'State of Affairs'

6

Perspectives on Knowledge Process[1] Adoption in Emerging Economies

*W*hat are Indian organizations doing about ramping up analytics capability—when is the right time to invest and why?

Motivation

This chapter is based on our research on the development of the analytics practice across various industries in India and the potential facilitators of and challenges to the adoption process. It also attempts to find reasons for seemingly lumpy development of Analytics in Indian organizations. It is felt that this may be a manifestation of an economy that is largely oriented towards production of knowledge and does not have an equally evolved consumption norm.

Additionally it will provide evidence, if any, of the diversity of analytic competency across organizations. In our opinion,

---

[1] Knowledge-driven process and Analytics, and data-driven process are terms that are used interchangeably.

such diversity in competency would indicate the heterogeneity in requirements and the need for better mapping of skills to business requirement in this industry.

The findings from India-based research may also resonate well with issues in other emerging economies. In that respect, our findings may be generalizable to other markets as well. The methodology adopted to conduct this study is described in Box 6.1.

Box 6.1   Details of the Survey

Overview of the Study Conducted

The study was conducted in the first half of 2015. It was exploratory in nature. Hence, we set about doing semi structured interviews with a cross section of industry practitioners in this domain to establish the taxonomy of issues that impact this domain.

Methodology

The study was conducted in two phases.

We conducted a total of 21 open ended discussions over a period of three months with business executives across industries. These respondents represented a diversity of functions and levels of seniority in their respective organizations. Their identities have been kept anonymous, a condition imposed by most of the respondents to agree to participate in this research. A set of guide questions were developed to initiate the discussion to ensure that most of the important dimensions of the industry were covered and the objectives of this research were met. Some of these dimensions emerged as a result of conducting our initial interviews and were included in subsequent interviews as well. The guidelines are mentioned in Appendix 5.

This work is different from most academic studies. It is largely exploratory and we initiated this project with practically no hypotheses. This was primarily due to our discomfort with little systematic work on this industry in India, which remains the focus of our present project.

Detailed Findings from the Business Executive Survey

A summary of the findings from the survey are presented below:

DISTINCT SECTORS OF ANALYTICS USAGE IN INDIA

There are three significant areas in which Analytics have developed in India. They are:

1. Offshore operations, which are largely driven by expertise and data that are imported, and function on the requirements of overseas businesses that support such operations.
2. Private sector financial institutions (primarily banks) that have started working with operational and transactional data to tailor make their operational decision making.
3. Digital and web space that generates large-scale data and can be easily manipulated to provide online feed on the decision changes required. But this is a fractional percentage of the total business transaction happening in India.[2] Our study does not capture this sector.
4. Apart from these three domains, the rest (diverse in nature) are also there trying to catch up with limited and many times unorganized sources of data that have the potential to yield—at best—modest results. We have made significant efforts here to check the potential of this sector.

---

[2] 'Evolution of E-commerce in India', http://www.pwc.in/assets/pdfs/publications/2014/evolution-of-e-commerce-in-india.pdf, accessed on 6 March 2014, 1325 hours (IST).

OVERALL ASSESSMENT OF ANALYTICS PROCESS DEVELOPMENT IN INDIAN ORGANIZATIONS BASED ON SURVEY

While details of our findings from various industry sectors are given in Table 6.1, we provide an overall summary of our perceptions based on these interactions.

1. **Non availability of comprehensive business data:** A prerequisite for effective data science application is the availability of data. It may be structured or semi-structured (or unstructured), nevertheless it is important that the coverage of the available data source should be close to complete and the variety of information available is broad enough to provide a wholesome view of the business phenomenon that is studied. None of these conditions are satisfied in many organizations. A secondary concern is the unorganized state of data in many organizations which makes it difficult to develop a systematic information plan to connect to decision-making processes.

   External information regarding markets and environment are the most difficult to acquire simply because there are few private or government agencies involved in the collection processes. Besides, the high cost of collection of data from relatively inaccessible parts of the country (rural markets, for instance) discourages investments in such initiatives.

   A consequent problem due to this non-availability of data is that the impact of data and its subsequent processing and insight on decision making remains largely muted and incomplete.

2. **Internal data in multiple and incompatible formats:** A second dimension of the complication for some organizations that have quality business data that gets generated as a part of the business operations, such as transaction data in banks and retail stores, is their

availability in different formats which causes significant problems of consolidation. Take, for instance, the banking and financial services institutions in India in the past decade and a half. There has been rapid development in computerization and automation of operations in most large public sector institutions. A consequence of this trend has been that recent data is available in standardized electronic formats, but their integration (or lack of it) with data available in legacy physical systems (read: paper formats) makes it difficult to apply any data science procedures reliably to glean insights for decision making.

3. **Dependency on heuristics for making decisions:** Given the above constraints, many business organizations remain steadfast on their dependency on heuristic business rules developed over long periods of experience and a firm connect 'with the ground'. People-driven decisions override attempts at standardization and the common refrain heard is that information is not available or is incomplete to substitute the 'gut feel' with the rigours of scientific models-based decision support systems. A notable example of such a focus is the role of branch operations in managing business operations in the field. It is very apparent in rural markets, where the role of the local branch is important, for taking both operational and at times strategic decisions. Here the lack of information is substituted by the 'look and feel' of the environment, which is only possible through a decentralized branch-based operations (our respondents from the banking and financial services sector corroborate with this view). A centralized process of decision making using data is therefore dispensed with and substituted by a people-led decentralized organization structure.

4. **Market growth and low competition hides the virtues of Analytics-driven precision in decisions:** The

'futility' of the analytics practice is also fuelled by the notion of the 'growing market syndrome'. Data scientists are supposed to extract business insights that act as a welcome succour in a highly mature and penetrated market. They are supposed to provide directions, refine decisions to hone in on the 'close to perfect' set of decisions for an environment. However, when the markets are in expanding phase, such extraction of precise insights from past transactions is not quite relevant. In such a situation the importance of factual evidences, based on past occurrences can easily be discounted since the growth in the market overrides the leakages of a sub-optimal decision. Precision in decision making or the lack of it has little consequence on the year-end performance of the organization since the overall market growth many times covers up for all such inefficiencies.

5. **Technology alone has limited potential to create impact:** Offshore operations seem to have relatively less problem due to non-availability of appropriate data infrastructure, but due to their operational bases being geographically distant from policy making units, suffer from lack of 'contextual relevance'. It was felt that embedded organizations with policy making and analytics support working in tandem and in close coordination, is necessary to ensure fructification of the true value of this domain. The domestic market imperatives being very different from the offshore challenges, does not help in ensuring a sufficient flow of trained human resources that can provide adequate domain expert knowledge in offshore operations.

6. **Globalization and cross pollination of ideas from multiple markets** have led to more awareness about the benefits of data-driven processes and the role of analytics. This is not a concern area, but an optimistic note for the future. More trained resources are available

Table 6.1 Summary of Findings Across Major Industries

Sector	Organizations Surveyed	Key Achievements	Challenges for the Future
Large public sector banks	1	a) Electronic data capture is mostly complete b) Data warehousing and report generation in progress	a) Do they need sophisticated analytics to support the banking function in a regulated market? b) Data resources are a mish-mash of electronic and old paper formats. It is very hard to organize them systematically.
Consumer products/ FMCG	3	a) High competition is compelling management to turn attention on analytics for better planning b) Better skills available with global movement of human resource	a) Scrappy data management and collection impedes effective output. b) Disconnect between analytics processors and users of its output; don't understand each other well.
Manufacturing/ engineering	3	a) Effective analytics capability available for focussed engineering applications b) Requisite skill set is available to support such analysis and inferencing	a) Non availability of comprehensive business databases (especially market related) hampers the true potential of activity.
ITES/offshore consultants/ captives	4	a) Developed processes and databases b) Supporting business decisioning with at least baseline support through reporting and analysis	a) Disconnect between Analytical prowess and business imperatives due to geographic distance. b) How to add value through Analytics?

(Continued)

(Continued)

Table 6.1 Summary of Findings Across Major Industries

Sector	Organizations Surveyed	Key Achievements	Challenges for the Future
Analytics consultants for Indian organizations	3	a) Provide analytical services (operational) for direct mailing and customer targeting activities. b) Reporting services for digital and web-based data	a) Not enough scale in the analytical services space. b) Not enough going on in strategic advisory through analytics due to scattered data bases in most indigenous organizations. c) Some organizations with large databases prefer to invest in an in-house consulting/analytical support. d) Forced to look overseas for offshore opportunities.
Financial services	4	a) New businesses are introducing relevant data collection architecture with the hope that they can collect relevant market information for future use. b) Some tactical level programs are supported with analytics	a) Felt need is low in organizations for analytics as the market continues to grow. b) Data exists in various forms: electronic, paper and sometimes in experience of employees. It is hard to put them together to run a reasonable analytical process for supporting decision making.

in the Indian market, which has led to some traction. Higher awareness has initiated some discussion and debate regarding the appropriateness of analytics to their specific context. Openness to ideas and technology that may help in data collection and management is noted as well. Such atmosphere was non-existent five years ago. The proliferation of offshore units that use sophisticated technology has also spurred interest in indigenous companies to initiate a review of their analytic potential.

What Did We Conclude?

While there are enough conversations happening in the domain of analytics, challenges in India-based operations are diverse and their origins are varied. Hence, there may not be one-resolution approach that is suitable for all organizations. However, it is easy to perceive that most India-based organizations may have similar issues of data organization that may be impeding their progression in the field of analytics. In Appendix 6, we have described our detailed investigations of a few organizations to substantiate this point.

THE ADOPTION OF ANALYTICS IN INDIAN ORGANIZATIONS: A PROPOSED MODEL

Based on the above summary of findings and some significant other insights from our survey, we propose a framework for adoption of Analytics in Indian firms. We have specifically not considered the issues identified in the ITES industry vertical, since, given its legacy, this industry is technically an 'implant' (service delivery extension) of overseas businesses and does not really merit being considered an out-and-out Indian industry.

We believe that the overarching drivers of Analytics adoption in organizations in India are:

1. **The availability and constraints of/perceived need for suitable data infrastructure:** This dimension has emerged as a primary driver/constraint of Analytics deployment across multiple industry verticals. Without availability and systematic management of information databases, significant deployment of analytics is not possible. 'Ease of access to data/market data', 'availability of methods to capture data' and 'availability of significant proportion of relevant data and in compatible formats' are some of the parameters identified by respondents that define this construct.

2. **Competitive intensity of the business environment:** This dimension, according to us is an important influencer of analytics adoption, as well. The critical need for competitive markets is a measured strategic and tactical response to market challenges. This need is perhaps not felt in the Indian market environment as much. Industry benchmarks are not seen to have been set on minimum required analytics capabilities for business performance. Rival organizations are not perceived to have made significant investments in analytics and hence its importance is not perceived. 'Regulated environment', 'high market growth rates' and 'low priority due to exigent needs elsewhere' are some of the parameters spelt out by respondents that define this construct.

Based on these two major identified constructs, we offer a model that explains the adoption of analytics in India. In this pursuit, we are significantly influenced by a similar model proposed by Germann et al.[3] While their paper looked at

---

[3] Germann, Frank, Lilien, Gary L., & Rangaswamy, Arvind (2012). 'Performance Implications of Deploying Marketing Analytics', *International Journal of Research in Marketing*, 30(2), 114–28.

the drivers of 'Analytics deployment' and subsequent 'firm performance', we have restricted ourselves in our study to examining the influencers of 'Analytics adoption/deployment' in firms. Our hunch is that evolving markets like India may require some more time to mature for them to realize the true impact of 'Analytics deployment' on 'firm productivity'.

The primary driver for adopting and productively using Analytics capabilities is the 'availability and access to data infrastructure' (positively related). This is supported by the views of our respondents in the survey. Taking support of the model proposed by Germann (2012), we propose that 'competitive intensity of the business environment' has a moderating role to this relationship (negative impact of low competition). While our claim is largely based on this previous research, we did obtain some evidence based on our discussion with some PSU bank executives who claimed that in their environment, 'higher order analysis was not needed, even if possible' because the banking regulator ensured a tight control over business options that could be considered.

'Availability and access to data infrastructure' investments in organizations are partly governed by:

1. Level of support from the top management ('Top Management Advocacy'). This construct is supported by parameters identified in our research such as 'felt need for analytics', 'easy availability of turnkey solutions' and 'exposure to global standards' in Analytics.
2. 'Awareness in the organization' about best practices across business environments also helps in facilitating faster adoption. Dimensions such as 'Global movement of Analytics talent' and also 'availability of Analytics vendors' who may provide comprehensive solutions to business analytics problems and 'low/high Analytics skill penetration', determine the level of awareness regarding the benefits of Analytics. There are some

inputs about how awareness about best global practices has had a direct impact on the adoption of analytics in Indian organizations.

The detailed model is presented in Figure 6.1.

Figure 6.1   Drivers of Analytics Adoption in Evolving Markets like India

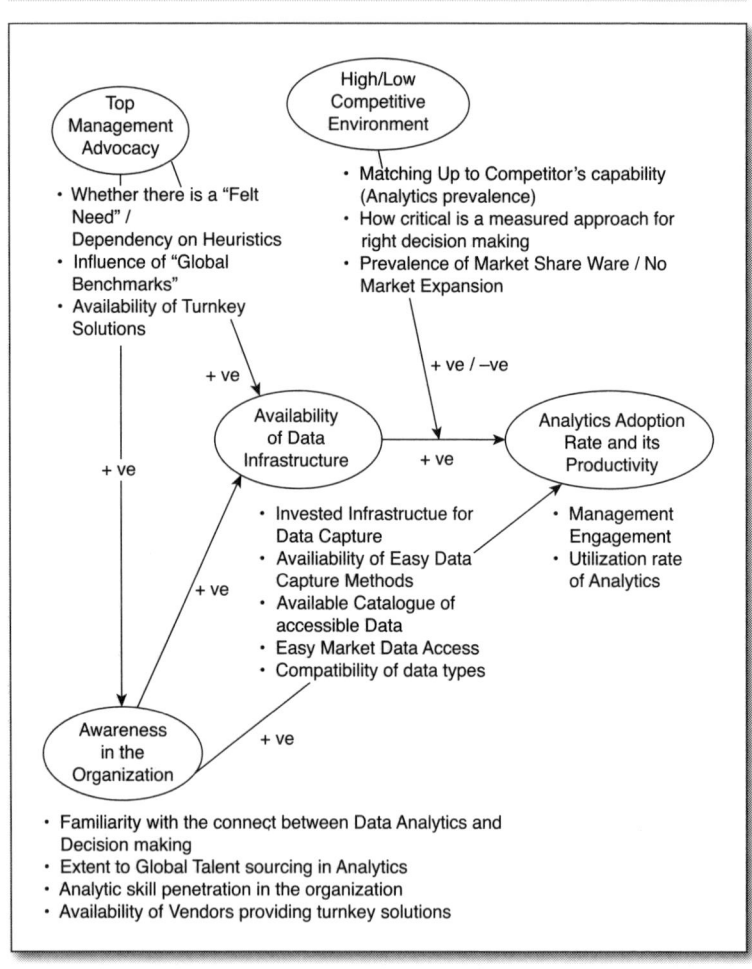

Unlike developed markets, the setting for the earlier cited work, we did not find material evidence of more refined constructs like the presence of 'Analytics culture' and 'Analytics skills' in organizations in our study. Perhaps the methods we employed in developing the proposition (qualitative study) and the evolutionary nature of the Indian business environment constrained our ability to identify these dimensions.

Ending Note

Our analytics journey in various Indian organizations ends here. Nascent no doubt, nevertheless, there are signs of adoption that will grow very quickly. What will be important is how business leaders sense the appropriate growth trajectory for building this capability in their own organizations. Context will vary and hence the trajectories and the pace may be different. However, if the focus is on achieving the business objectives, and the data and analyses are aligned to the final objectives that need to be supported, organizations will not go awry in their pursuit to develop effective analytic capabilities.

Our experience also shows that infrastructure alone does not build an analytic climate in organizations. It must be preceded with some hunger creation with 'best practices' developed through useful analyses in different parts of the organization's ecosystem. Only then can the infrastructure facilitate the faster adoption of analytics across organizations.

Postscript

Our objective in writing this book was primarily to address issues faced by decision makers (mainly in emerging economies like India) while dealing with a relatively new organizational process called Analytics. While the topic has created enormous interest in the practicing world, we firmly believe that most of the insights being developed in the field are focussed on the role of the analysts and little, if at all, is being developed that would be insightful to, (a) a decision maker, (b) a consumer of insights and (c) an investor of analytics process.

Our attempt was to fill up this gap in the literature by identifying the focus areas for an organizational leader, to drive effectiveness in an analytics function. The first five chapters and the Introduction of the book deal with these issues and approaches to deal with some of them. The next chapter is solely focussed on compiling the voice of the industry experts and their priorities and concerns.

In conclusion, we want to bust some common myths regarding Analytics:

MYTH # 1: ANALYTICS IS ABOUT A TECHNOLOGY (PLATFORM)-BASED CAPABILITY IN ORGANIZATIONS

Nothing can be farther from truth. Technology is at best a facilitator of effective Analytics in organizations. The process has to be guided, driven and evaluated by business managers continuously. The larger role of technology (automation) comes much later when the process becomes standardized and need not depend as much upon human intervention.

MYTH # 2: ANALYTICS IS ABOUT DATA SCIENCE

Here's another fable that is worth dismissing at the earliest. True, data science (computer-based modelling and statistical analysis) is a facilitator and a good one in certain domain with large data bases, however, like automation, data science expertise is not the uber solution for all Analytics requirements for organizations.

MYTH # 3: ANALYTICS SHOULD BE A SPECIALIZED, STAND-ALONE CAPABILITY IN ORGANIZATIONS

This is, again, not generalizable for all organizations. At different stages of evolution, Analytics may be 'embedded' to a business or a 'specialized' stand-alone function. For instance, in the early stage of evolution, embedded functions may lead to better appreciation of the value of Analytics by the ultimate user community in the organization.

Also, the nature of some businesses may require continuous interfacing with analytic teams. In this case, embedded structures are more effective. Pursuit of new innovations and 'better' models, which have a greater role of technology, may trigger the formation of specialized Analytic units manned by qualified data scientists.

MYTH # 4: ANALYTICS 'SUBSTITUTES' FOR BUSINESS ACUMEN

Surely it does not. However, it may help better decision making by providing consistent findings from data. It can help in validating hunches and refuting subjective claims with evidence from data. The necessary condition is that appropriate data should be available to support such processes.

We hope the contents of this book have accomplished the above. To summarize, leadership in organizations involved with developing internal capabilities in Analytics may focus squarely on the following:

1. Mapping available data resources in the organization to their potential utility in supporting key business decisions.

2. Developing the analysis framework (plan) that is needed to convert these important data into useful information that feeds into decision making.

3. Creating an evaluation criterion to measure the benefit of the information (analysis) on business performance/ decision making.

4. Building effective communication skills in its analytics professionals to project the benefits of the process output in a form relevant for decision makers.

5. Assessing the appropriateness of the existing (prospective) analytic infrastructure to facilitate the above.

6. Staying clear of infrastructure investment decisions without undergoing the planning steps mentioned above. Many organizations have made this error in judgement.

We wanted to emphasize the difference between process management of Analytics and the outcome/objective management approach. Our book focuses on the issues related to monitoring outcome and benefits obtained from running an Analytics operation with an eye to improving business performance. This distinction has been repeatedly brought out in various parts of the book.

Lastly, we hope that the reader is able to get a mix of both directive oriented knowledge as well as perspectives of varied stakeholders in this domain. Hopefully, in the process we are able to achieve a unique position for this book in the slew of technical books available on this subject matter.

APPENDIX 1

RAILROAD CLEANING SERVICE (CASE)

One summer afternoon in July 1995, Terry West sat in his small office in suburban Rye, New York, thinking about his financial success in the past four years since he had launched Railroad Cleaning Service (RCS). Business looked good with sales touching almost $2 million annually. With no signs of significant direct competition in the market, Terry was optimistic of yet another year of good fortune with a high growth rate of around 45 percent. He wondered why no one else was venturing into his business model given that it had made such an impact in the market place. He just could not believe his good luck.

The Commuting New Yorker

Terry finished his bachelor's in Actuarial Sciences from Tulane University in New Orleans and headed to New York City (NYC) with the dream of striking gold in the field of business and commerce in the big city. It was the fall of 1988, when armed with a $32,000 per annum job in NYC, Terry took up quarters in its northern suburbs in Greenwich, CT.

Each workday Terry would be up by about 6:30 AM, and would barely have time to make a cup of coffee, grab his business suit and somehow find his way into it, only to hurriedly head out of the front door of his small apartment to catch the 7:10 Stamford local train on NYC's Metro-North rail line. The Greenwich train station was thankfully just around the corner from his apartment block and reaching it just in time to catch the train was usually not a problem. The Stamford local train would disgorge its passengers at NYC's main terminus, the Grand Central at 8:25 AM, just enough time for Terry to hail a taxi to his place of work by 8:45 AM. Terry worked at a small insurance firm in mid-town Manhattan, and his boss did not like him being late to work. This was, after all, Terry's first job after school and he meant to keep it to save enough money for Graduate School.

Work and commuting to and from office consumed most of Terry's life for the next 4–5 years. Most work days, Terry would return home at about 9:00 PM, spent by the day's commute and would have just enough stamina to grab a frozen dinner from the refrigerator and put it on the gas grill to broil. That would be his dinner.

Weekends were more relaxed and primarily meant to catch up on sleep. Although the week had a punishing schedule, it also meant weekends would be consumed in getting the laundry done, fixing the house and yard for homeowners and attending to the countless chores that suburban living imposed upon New Yorkers.

To sum up the life of a typical suburban New Yorker, it did not exactly sound very exciting. More so for a young, single male like Terry West trying to make a future in the 'Big Apple'.

The Idea

Over the years that Terry used the Metro train service to commute to New York, he had lots of time to ponder aimlessly during the hour-fifteen minute ride to and from NYC. Like him, countless New Yorkers living in suburban Westchester county, eastern counties of New Jersey that bordered on Manhattan and Long Island travelled to and from work and on an average spent 3 hours travelling each day. That amounted to an average of 15 hours of travel time each week. With over 4.5 million commuters travelling to Manhattan from various locations in Long Island (Long Island Railroad), Westchester County (Metro-North Railroad) and New Jersey (NJ Transit), there were many whose life was short of one critical thing: time. Like Terry, they spent way too much time travelling and hence, once they were back home, they had too little time to attend to their daily personal chores.

One day in June 1991, while travelling to work on the Stamford Local, Terry finally made up his mind. He decided to quit his job in the insurance firm as well as his dream of becoming a successful business executive and launched his company—Railroad Cleaning Service.

With a $2500 investment from his bank savings account, Terry rented space at the Greenwich railroad station from the Metro-North Company and set up a kiosk. Every morning from 6:45 AM, Terry would man his kiosk, which served as a drop-off counter for dirty shirts. Commuters travelling to New York would drop off their shirts to be taken care by Terry's laundry service. The kiosk would remain open until 9:30 AM for people to drop off their laundry.

By mid-morning, Terry would cart the entire lot to the local laundry facility in Greenwich to be washed, cleaned and ironed. The lot would be ready for return by 4:00 PM for Terry to return to his kiosk at the station, just in time for the start of the evening rush hour traffic from NYC. Normally the kiosk would remain open for laundry pick-up until 9:00 PM to cater to the late commuters from the city.

Business was uncertain at first, but picked up quite steadily after the first 15 days. In fact, Terry had to get a temporary help within the first month to help him with the growing demand.

From a regular customer, 'This is very much wanted around here… I mean,… who's got the time to get the laundry done at the end of the day... and I don't have enough shirts to get me through the week,... this is what was required... just great !!!'

The premium charged by Terry for his service ranged from 10 percent to as much as 40 percent compared to the charges at the regular Laundromat. Prices were higher for delicate items. Commuters did not mind paying up for the service provided, especially since it reduced the aggravation of getting one's cleaning job done at the end of the day or on weekends.

Within a few months of operations, Terry was doing about $1500 of business a day. Initially, he accepted men's shirts for laundry, but eventually he began accepting women's dresses too. Soon he realized that his beat up Chevrolet sedan was becoming too small to cart the laundry over to the local Laundromat, so he leased a pick-up truck to relieve the pressure off his sedan.

A year from the start of the operations, Terry had bought out the Laundromat, in the way of backward integration of his business. He had hired three permanent helps to man his kiosk and had also opened two new pick-up kiosks at Stamford, CT and Rye, NY to cater to additional customers. He was also eyeing the Long Island Railroad system to expand his business into other routes in the New York suburban transport system. He realized that the potential of his idea was enormous and that he had to quickly move in to capture the potential market before anyone else could copy his idea.

By March 1995, Railroad Cleaning Service was a $3 million turnover company, employing 45 full-time employees and operating 15 railroad stations across Westchester County, Long Island and New Jersey. Competition has been slow to get in and Terry has been effectively deterring entry by opening kiosks at high density station which were at least

30 miles from Grand Central station. In July 1994, a similar service sprang up at Trenton station on the NJ Transit route.

Terry could not fulfil his dream of becoming a business whiz kid, but he sure does have the business acumen to generate profits out of unusual business ideas.

Problem to be addressed in this situation:

If you are a potential competitor of Terry West, how would you plan a research project to evaluate the option of entering the market?

APPENDIX 2

ABV TYRE COMPANY (CASE)

ABV is a tyre manufacturing company primarily selling two-wheeler tyres to industrial buyers (like Bajaj, LML, Hero Honda, etc.). The company has non-existent presence in the replacement market with minimal brand recall in the market place. It also wanted to protect its domination in the industrial market, fearing that a low brand-recall in the replacement market would backfire someday in their industrial market share. The company wanted to develop a growth strategy to expand its replacement market share.

The company's previous experiences of vehicle inter-mediates (components of two wheelers) indicated that pull strategies to develop markets would be difficult because of the low levels of customer involvement. But, tyre being more visible could be among the 'higher' involvement inter-mediates and hence subject to some evaluation of quality by the buyer. The type of Influences (and Influencers) on decision making and involvement levels may also differ across two wheeler segments (bikes and scooters). See Figure A2.1.

A structure of the customer decision-making process is given:

Various strategic initiatives have been used to reach the target groups by various tyre manufacturers. The dealers are targeted through direct communication, sales process, service and policy schemes. Mechanics/influencers are reached through media positioning and direct schemes. Positioning, mass media and PR are used to interact with the end users.

Figure A2.1   Influencers in the Buying Process

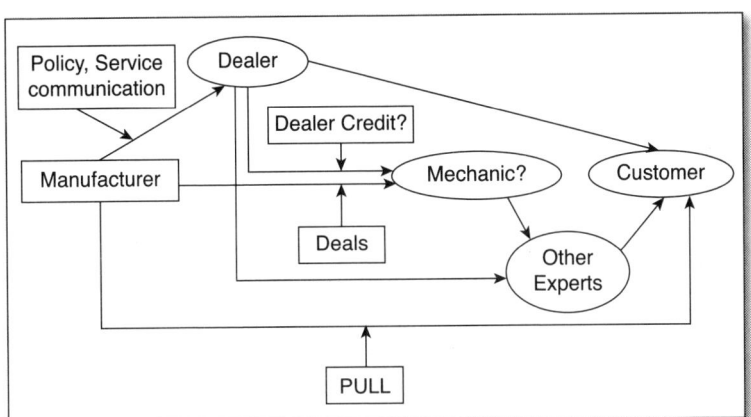

In the overall tyre market, ABV has a miniscule share since it specializes in two wheeler tyres only (and concentrates in the industrial markets). The big players in the market like MRF, Ceat, draw their strength from being multi-vehicle tyre manufacturers which include truck, car and two wheelers. ABV has a disadvantage retailing two wheeler tyres in the replacement market where its formidable competitors use the leverage of having a complete product line. ABV's strength lies in having a leading presence in the industrial buyer segment of the two wheeler tyre market; hence, it has an opportunity to cater to a significant number of buyers of new two wheelers.

Past Attempts at Understanding Customers

Past research by ABV on consumer preferences have been rather sketchy and market information has been collected on an ad hoc basis. There is no evidence of any extensive study conducted on consumers and most of the theories going around in the company are based on hunches and 'gut feel'.

In summary, the marketing department did not have a consistent and researched understanding of what drove tyre sales and how did customers go about buying two wheeler tyres. Some probing by a set of external consultants revealed that marketing and sales had a different version of what product attributes were important to the customer.

It should also be noted here that ABV has a state of the art manufacturing facility which includes a modern tyre testing lab. Most of their tyres compare well vis-à-vis their competitors' tyres in lab tests and road tests conducted by ABV. The quality of tyres is judged on wear-rate of the tyre, which is measured with a calibration device after certain pre-specified usage.

Market Coverage

ABV Tyres has sales operations in the North, West and South zones. Export sales are close to 10 percent of total sales. Central office and factory are located in Coimbatore, Tamil Nadu. ABV is affiliated to a large south-based auto ancillary distribution network. This affiliation provides the advantage of cross-selling with other ancillaries as well as the potential of better utilization of the common distribution network.

To formulate a growth strategy, ABV felt the need to understand:

1. the relative impact of customers and influencers on sales, what drives each type of customer to buy a brand and each type of influencer to push a brand,
2. what cues a good tyre and a good tyre company, and

3. the gaps in the strengths/weaknesses of its brand vis-à-vis competition both in the OE vehicle buying segment as well as the replacement segment.

Problem for resolution: Identify the 'true' problem that needs resolution and prepare an approach to solve it.

APPENDIX 3

MARKETING MIX MODELLING

Customer Tracking services, such as the ones maintained by large research agencies like AC Nielsen and IRI in the United States, provide information not only about consumer attitudes but also their actual behaviour on an ongoing basis. Behavioural data is considered more useful for developing strategy since it directly reflects on business performance rather than conventional slice-in-time customer surveys. This has led to the emergence of marketing research techniques designed for planning future marketing initiatives, against the more traditional role of merely reporting 'nice-to-know' customer reactions in posterity.

Prediction modelling became a widely used methodology to calibrate marketing mix to positively impact customer response. This trend became popular specifically in the consumer packaged goods (CPG) industry in the United States with large organisations such as Philip Morris, Coke, Pepsi, etc., adopting these models for resolving both their strategic and more tactical level decisions.

A very widely used managerial decision support system (DSS) based on prediction modelling of customers' transaction level data is the volume (market share) decomposition analysis. It has evolved, over a period, into a standard diagnostic tool for marketing managers in developed markets to assess the effectiveness of their marketing programmes. It also helps the manager to evaluate the attractiveness of alternate marketing strategies and therefore is an effective aid in his/her decision making. The analysis provides a logical basis to the manager to compute the differential impact of a firm's advertising strategies and sales strategy vis-à-vis its competitors on the market share of its brands. The total sale of the firm's brand is decomposed into base sales (shown as grey colour area in Figure A3.1) and incremental sales (shown as dotted area in Figure A3.1). The base sale is driven by the long-term equity of the firm and is a reflection of its decisions in the past vis-à-vis its competitors. Whereas incremental sales of the firm is influenced by the short-term marketing activity (tactics) of the firm as well as its competitors and helps managers evaluate the effectiveness of various tactics.

The DSS uses the β-coefficients (average impact on sales) of each marketing programme estimated from a sophisticated choice model using statistical techniques such as multinomial logit and regression, to decompose the total brand market share into individual components that are directly attributable to specific marketing activities (price reductions, promotion packs, freebies, etc.). The consumer choice model is an integral part of developing such DSS and is extensively used in marketing research in developed

Figure A3.1   Decomposition of Volume into Base and Incremental Components

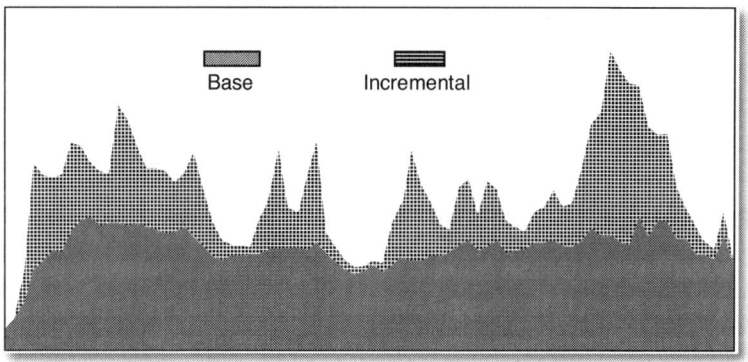

markets to identify real drivers of market performance. Ideally, a choice model requires an input of customer databases covering attributes related to demographic (age, education, etc.), psychometric (attitudes, etc.) and marketing mix variables (price, promotion, advertising, display, etc.) of all competing brands in a product category over large number of purchase occasions from a representative customer sample. Customer tracking services in the developed markets have developed expertise in collecting and managing these types of data on a continuous basis. Depending on the richness of available data (measured in terms of the number of customer-related and market-related data collected) the incremental sales in Figure A3.1 can further be decomposed to find incremental sales due to price, promotion, trade discounts and short-term advertising or image-building effort of the firm (refer Figure A3.2). Such decomposition of volume/share into component shares can help managers objectively identify the cause of gain/loss in market share and segregate successful strategies from the rest.

Moreover, it helps in diagnosing the effect of actions taken by competitors in the same period. Development of such planning tools have had an enormous impact in terms of fine

Figure A3.2 'Due to' Analysis using Marketing Mix Modelling

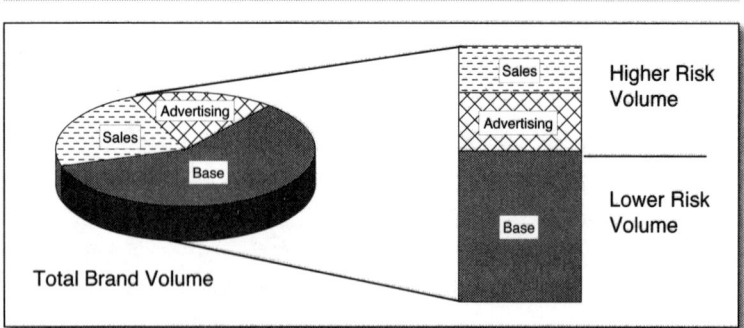

tuning strategic and tactical planning activities in the CPG sector in the United States.

A conceptually similar DSS has been developed recently at the Indian Institute of Management (IIM), Ahmedabad. The system is unique since it is built on consumer panel data available in the Indian market environment. Information from consumer panel maintained by a large research agency which tracks consumer purchases, retail audit information from Nielsen which provides pricing and promotional data, and consumers' attitudinal information regarding brands collected from an ongoing survey-based panel are the inputs into this DSS. The data was made available for this pilot project by a marketing organisation in FMCG sector. The objective of this pilot was to develop a decision model which would help marketing managers diagnose the impact of brand-building initiatives vis-à-vis field level selling initiatives in the overall performance of the brand (market share). It is purported that this is the first step towards building a powerful diagnostic as well as prognostic tool for Indian mangers.

The project replicated the steps described earlier with regards to the estimation of a consumer choice model and subsequent decomposition of the share into parts attributable to each marketing mix element. At a preliminary step, this system can help managers decompose the total market share to base level share and incremental share (refer Figure A3.3).

The incremental share is largely driven by the short-term sales efforts of the firm. The ability to decompose total share into components that can be specifically attributed to every marketing tactic used is directly related to the amount of details that are captured in the input data regarding the specific marketing activities initiated in the market place. Given the limitations in the scope of data collection in the Indian market, it is not possible to execute the volume decomposition at the level of granularity obtained with similar

Figure A3.3   Decomposition of Market Share in Indian Context Based on Model

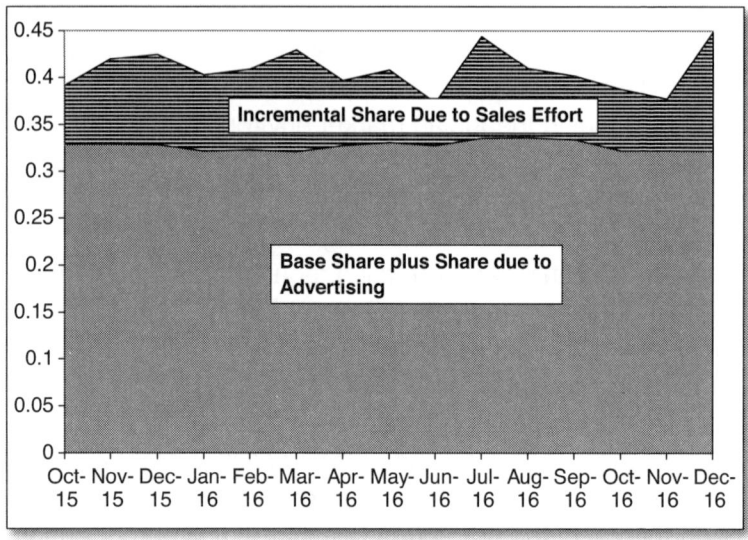

types of data collected from the United States. It is anticipated that with improvements in the collection techniques and increase in demand for more detailed record of market level activities, the outputs can be significantly improved.

Managerial Uses of Volume Decomposition Methodology

As a diagnostic tool the DSS can help managers evaluate their periodic investments in various marketing activities vis-à-vis the corresponding performance (volume or market share) attributable to it. Specifically, it helps identify the relative importance of advertising and sales efforts in achieving the ultimate sales. Table A3.1 illustrates an example by which annual expenses incurred in various types of marketing activities are compared with the volume/market share of

Table A3.1   Contribution Versus Efficiency

Marketing Activity	Expenditure (₹ Lacs)	Market Share Impact (%)	Cost Efficiency
TV Advertising	10	30	0.33
Print Advertising	1	2	0.50
Radio Advertising	2	1	2.00
Price Cut	2	1	2.00
Freebee	0.5	2	0.25
Joint Promotion	1	4	0.25

the brand attributable to the specific activity. This provides a powerful basis to evaluate marketing activities on an efficiency measure.

It can also foster more efficient resource allocation for future by identifying effective versus ineffective market development initiatives. As competitive marketing environments become too complex for the manager to evaluate at a holistic level, the model output can provide enough flexibility for the manager to compare alternative strategies after accounting for the complexities in market dynamics. The scenario builder (Figure A3.4) developed on the basis of the model output provides insights about probable outcome due to alternative marketing initiatives for managers to get a 'feel' on what may drive improved performance of their brands. This tool can also evaluate possible competitive reactions to changes in one's own marketing policies. The net result of all changes is portrayed in terms of likely market share of various brands.

Volume (share) decomposition models and their applications have fairly widespread use in the brand and sales management activities of CPG companies in the United States. At a generic level, these applications help managers improve

Figure A3.4   Scenario Builder

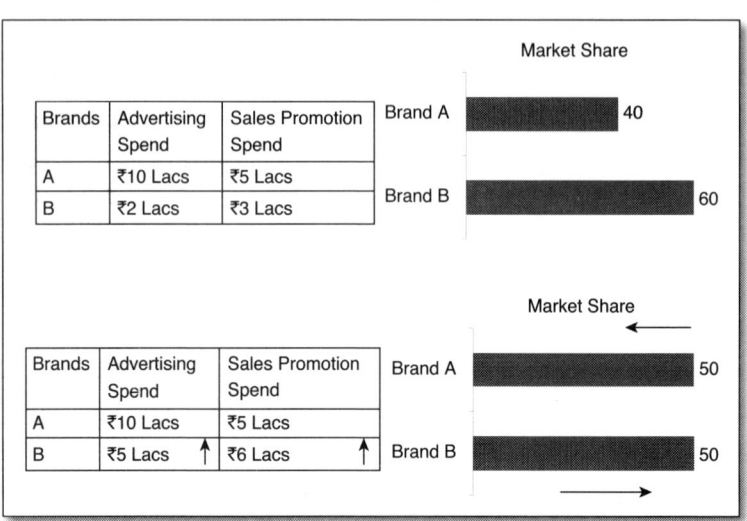

the consistency of their decisions by acting as a 'bouncing board' to validate their own subjective assessments based on their field experience. More specifically, they assist in developing insights about market dynamics in managerial environments where such intuition is lacking. There is however, the danger of relying too much on the market share forecasts computed by the models on making decisions for the future. Managers must exercise caution while drawing inferences based on the model output since the constraints imposed by the standard techniques of developing mathematical models limit to some extent their 'representativeness' to the real market conditions.

The simplicity of interpretation of volume/share decomposition is the primary reason for its widespread use as a standard tool for making brand and sales management decisions in the United states. Our experience at IIM Ahmedabad in building such models using Indian data has provided some very encouraging results towards developing user-friendly decision support tools.

The relevance of these models in Indian context is beyond doubt. A significant contribution in marketing diagnostics is possible using these models to attribute good/bad performance to specific functional initiatives such as brand-building programmes or ground level sales development activities. While it is easy to point out some negative ramifications of such management reporting, such as it being used to identify 'scapegoats' in the organisation to account for poor performance, it is obvious that the utility of this tool is enormous if used meaningfully to invest in the appropriate market-building activities in the long run. Figure A3.3 clearly depicts a real-life example of the sales function acting as support to the more significant brand-building activities (viewed in terms of proportion of share attributable to each activity group). Our experience shows that this would be true for many product categories in the Indian market where opportunities for market growth and product differentiation are still significant. In the developed markets such as the United States, many product categories exhibit just the opposite characteristic. Market maturity reduces differentiation across brands and the larger proportion of brand market share of leading brands is vulnerable to competitive selling pressures. This fact highlights the predominant role of brand equity building in the Indian context compared to more myopic sales promotional strategies.

Market share decomposition models can be developed for any appropriate geographic market definition—at the country level, a region-specific or city-specific level or even a city-part specific level. The market definition for model development is primarily driven by appropriateness (accounting for the heterogeneity of consumers across various market, and also varied marketing programmes run in various geographic territories) and the availability of adequate consumer data at various defined market levels. If the richness in the data source is adequate, such models can be developed for various customer segment levels (as opposed to geographic markets) to evaluate effectiveness of marketing programmes across various demographic and psychographic segments. A critical barrier to large-scale usage of these models in India is the non-availability of adequate resource such as a detailed customer database. Managers have expressed interest in such analytical processes and confirm the usefulness of the outputs emanating from such models. However, most organisations lack resources to build large-scale customer databases on their own to initiate such modelling ventures. This is an opportunity for a consortium of like-minded managers across firms to organise and develop a syndicated customer data service for initiating such prognostic marketing research activities.

APPENDIX 3A

NOTE ON REGRESSION MODELS

Ordinary Least Squares (OLS) regression models are very prolifically used prediction models in practice. The basic requirement for developing these models is an outcome variable that is measured on a continuous scale (interval or ratio) and juxtaposed on the outcome variable should be some relevant predictor (exogenous) variables also measured usually on a continuous scale.

The model-building process attempts to fit a linear additive function (we assume this mathematical form) of the predictor variables to the outcome variable. In the process, the weights (coefficients) of the predictor variables are determined in such a way that the summation of the variables (adjusted by their weights) has a value closest to the value of the outcome variable (the best fit equation).

The closer the fit is to the actual data (higher r-square), the better is the chance that the equation will be able to predict outcomes based on values of the input (predictor) variables better. However, there is no guarantee that the models will continue to predict well, unless the nature of the data remains largely the same.

The standardized coefficient (the magnitude) signifies the importance of the variable in determining the value of the outcome. The sign (+ve or −ve) determines the nature of the relationship between the outcome and the variable. For instance, the weight associated with the price variable in determining sales will normally have a negative value, signifying an opposite relationship between price and sales (see Figure A3A.1).

Figure A3A.1   Associations in Regression

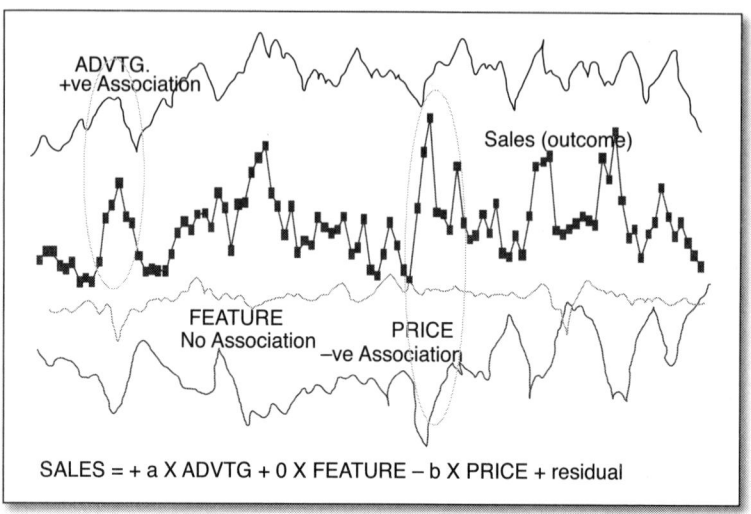

The model which is developed on a training sample is tested across multiple validation sample to check on the reliability of its prediction power before it is approved for use.

Predictive power can be increased in the training sample by using more complex mathematical functions instead of a simple additive linear regression model. Non-linear functions, sector-wise functional forms of different order, incorporating discontinuity in the functions are various ways to customize the prediction model given the nature of distribution of the outcome variable in the training sample. However, like in separation models (logistic models), too much customization may not be useful from reliability of prediction perspective, since many such models are not seen to perform up to mark in independent validation exercises. Hence, the seasoned practitioner's tussle is to match the customization of the model to the need for reliable predictability. This exercise is usually context driven and depends on the nature of data that is used to build and validate models.

Predictive models are relatively easier to specify compared to diagnostic models that identify associations between profile variables and the outcome. In the latter, the identification of a logical association is more important (not reducing the importance of predictability as much). Reliable prediction is not the main aim of developing these models as much as being able to identify the causation of a certain behaviour outcome.

Developing diagnostic regression models require a curious mix of technical acumen and contextual familiarity to pick the right profile variables, ensure that the impact of each variable is exactly measured without the confounding due to colinearity[1] in the profile variables. This is as much an art as it is a science and it is left to the experienced analyst to take the right calls.

Linear regression models are widely discussed and literature is openly available. We would encourage the reader to seek appropriate references for a more detailed exposition of these models.

---

[1] Multicollinearity problems in regression models: Consult a technical book on regression to understand the problem and its probable resolution.

APPENDIX 4

LOGIT MODELLING: A NOTE

We just touched upon Regression Analysis and OLS in the previous section. Just to reiterate, regression analysis is used to build a causal relationship between a dependent variable, say sales volume, and a set of independent variables, say price, discount, advertising, store display. A causal relationship is more like a one-way influencer relationship—price or advertising changes have an impact on the changes in sales volume in the retail store. However, the reverse is not proven. Significantly, the business impact is estimated as changes in a continuous variable either in monetary terms (total volume worth in rupees) or, in the actual number of units or net weight sold (total number of kg). The dependent variable is interval scaled (loosely described as continuous variable).

The problem becomes somewhat intriguing when the dependent variable does not have the elements of an interval scale. For instance, if instead of sales volume of a particular brand of soap we had to examine the effect of competitive measures on the consumer's proclivity towards a brand, exhibited in terms of her choice; say, if the price differential (difference in price of the two brands of the same pack size) is changed from ₹50 to ₹30, what impact does it have on the consumer's inclination to buy *Dove* over a competing brand, say, *Fiama*? (To keep the problem manageable, in our stylized environment, let us assume for now that the market has only these two brands to offer.) Of course, we can certainly incorporate other significant effects of the market that influence the choice decision, but the point that we are making here is that there is a structural change in the model from the one we were describing for volume changes. Instead of sales volume, we have a nominal variable — choice between *Dove* and *Fiama* as a dependent variable. The independent variable is also modified from price to price differential. Philosophically, the problem remains what we have solved before in regression analysis, except that the structure has changed.

How Do We Build a Model to Predict Brand Choice?

While the actual outcome in our stylized scenario is either choosing *Dove* or *Fiama* (one cannot choose both in our example), the model which we use to model this zero-sum game is stochastic. The choice of *Dove* is denoted by the following probability:

$$\Pr (Dove) = \{\exp (U_{Dove}) / (\exp(U_{Dove}) + \exp (U_{Fiama}))\} \qquad (1)$$

(exp. means exponential).

'Pr (*Dove*)' is the estimated probability that the *Dove* brand will be chosen by the customer on a particular shopping occasion. The probability is dependent on the exp (Utility) of both brands. It is not very difficult to imply that the probability of choosing *Dove* is dependent not only on its own utility, but also on utility provided by the competitive brand. Hence, the final outcome is a derivative of the relative perceived strength of the brands in a particular shopping occasion.

Similarly, the probability of choosing *Fiama* is

1− Pr(Dove), that is,

$$\Pr (Fiama) = \{\exp (U_{Fiama}) / (\exp(U_{Dove}) + \exp (U_{Fiama}))\} \qquad (2)$$

The two probabilities add up to one, indicating that these are the only two options that the customer can execute. However, it is easy to incorporate the possibility of many other options, and also the possibility of 'non-purchase' in the model to make it more realistic and generalizable.

Now let us turn our attention to the utility function. Suffice to say that the Utility for each brand can be represented as (illustrative):

$$U_{Dove} = a_{Dove} + b_1 * (Price)_{Dove} + b_2 * (Discount)_{Dove} + b_3 *$$
$$(Other\ Marketing\ Mix\ elements)_{Dove} \tag{3}$$

The utility is composed of some specific *Dove* related dimensions, say product attributes (we refer to them as 'a') and, some marketing mix variables specifically attributable to the brand. The 'b's are similar to the regression coefficients that one measures in OLS; to us they are more like the impact of the particular parameter on the utility, while economists casually would put it as elasticity.

To complete the argument, *Fiama* will have its own utility function, with parameters that pertain to the brand ('a', price, discount and other marketing mix variables, etc.). The impact coefficients 'b's are the same as the ones in the *Dove* utility function. Like in regression models, the purpose of this statistical model (also called the **Logit model**) is to estimate the 'b's or the impact coefficients.

It is not very difficult to perceive that choice probability (Pr) of a particular brand is not only dependent upon its own set of parameters (marketing mix or others), but also on the alternative's (competitive) values for the same parameters. Mathematically-tuned readers will appreciate our attempt to transform the original equation (1) into the following:

$$Pr\ (Dove) = \{exp(U_{Dove} - U_{Fiama}) / (exp(U_{Dove} - U_{Fiama}) + 1)\}, \tag{4}$$

where

$$(U_{Dove} - U_{Fiama}) = (a_{Dove} - a_{Fiama}) + b_1 * ((Price)_{Dove} - (Price)_{Fiama}) +$$
$$b_2 * ((Discount)_{Dove} - (Discount)_{Fiama}) + b_3 * (difference\ of\ other$$
pertinent measures across the brands)

Similarly,

$$Pr\ (Fiama) = \{(1) / (exp(U_{Dove} - U_{Fiama}) + 1)\}$$

Hopefully, this transformation will help appreciate the fact that choice of brand is dependent on not only what a particular brand's marketing mix is, but also on what the competition is up to (hence, the predictors are transformed as differences). After estimating the coefficients, one can use this mathematical formulation to simulate what the choice probabilities may be if one changes some parameter (within reasonable ranges) with respect to competition.

Recapitulating the significance of the impact coefficients ('b's): The magnitude and direction (positive or negative) of the coefficients will determine which parameter (for example, marketing mix or brand specific), rather the difference in the parameter values of the two brands, will impact the relative share of *Dove versus Fiama*.

Estimating Logit Models

Recalling the normal regression case, OLS technique uses the principle of *minimizing* the variance (squared difference of the actual volume to that obtained by the predictor function). In a brand choice example, or in the general case, whenever the dependent variable is categorical, the data comes in the form of the category selected (for example, the person chose *Dove* or *Fiama* on a certain purchase occasion). This is more like assigning a probability of choice of 1 for the chosen brand and zero for the brand not chosen. Logit estimation (maximum likelihood method) tries to estimate coefficients that will *maximize* the probability of choosing the brand that was actually chosen on *every* purchase occasion (note the stress on word 'every').

For a live example, if one is given a string of purchases and the corresponding marketing mix differentials for each purchase occasion:

Occasion 1	Brand chosen	*Fiama*
Occasion 2	Brand chosen	*Dove*
Occasion 3	Brand chosen	*Dove*
Occasion 4	Brand chosen	*Fiama*
Occasion 5	Brand chosen	*Fiama*
Occasion 6	Brand chosen	*Dove*

In this example, the Logit model will try to estimate the coefficients such that:

The likelihood function or the joint probability of all six purchases are maximized: Pr(*Fiama*) * Pr(*Dove*) * Pr(*Dove*) * Pr(*Fiama*) * Pr(*Fiama*) * Pr(*Dove*).

It is now worth talking about applications of this model. Obviously, it does not take much thinking to anticipate that the entire brand choice prediction is done using this technique. Market research organizations such as Information Resources Inc. (IRI) and AC Nielsen Corporation (ACN) collect individual household level data (panel data) from a large representative sample of households (about 40,000 each) in the United States. ACN has a similar panel in India as well. Data such as brands bought, amount bought, price paid, any discounts obtained, coupons used and any store displays seen by the customer are recorded for every purchase occasion. This database provides a rich source of information to the CPG industry in the United States on consumer price elasticity, brand loyalty and product assortment issues. Logit modelling is a common statistical technique used to develop choice prediction models and build further complex choice-quantity models (what brands do consumers buy and how much do they buy based on the marketing mix variables as well as product and consumer attributes such as loyalty and value).

The example that we discussed above is the case of two choices. Two choice logit models are appropriately called binary logit or logistic regression. Usually, in situations where one brand is a market leader and one would like to study the effect of competitive pricing on the market share of the leader, binary logit is the way to go. (Note that the estimated probability which is obtained from the logit model can be construed as estimated market share too.)

The world is far more complex than what can be accommodated in a binary logit model. Most choice situations have multiple alternatives or brands. In situations like these, an extension of the binary logit is used, which is widely known as the **multinomial logit** (MNL). Even more complicated models, such as Hierarchical (Nested) logits attempt to model both 'Direct' and 'Indirect' competitors, which are models closer to the reality. However, more realistic models are also complicated and harder to estimate and additionally do not have the intuitive 'feel' that simpler models provide. Hence, in practice most applications of logit modelling are reduced to a two-state case (also popularly termed as logistic regression).

The Polytomous Logit Model

A close variant of the above logit model (also called Conditional Logit) is the polytomous binary logit model. Instead of option (brand) specific predictor variables, the respondent characteristics (demographics, attitude, etc.) are used to predict their choice outcome. For instance, the probability of choosing *Dove* will be,

$$\text{Pr} \, (Dove) = \{\exp \, (U_{Respondent}) \, / \, (\exp(U_{Respondent}) + 1)\}, \tag{5}$$

where $U_{Respondent} = \Sigma \, [\beta \, X \, (\text{respondent characteristics such as age, income, attitude, etc.})]$
   Similarly,

$$\text{Pr} \, (Fiama) = \{1 \, / \, (\exp(U_{Respondent}) + 1)\}.$$

Note that the 'β' coefficients determine the strength and direction of influence of the respondent characteristic on the propensity to choose the alternative (*Dove*). As earlier, the probabilities of choice for the two options add up to one. The direction of influence that the characteristics have on the propensity to choose the other brand (*Fiama*) will all be opposite to their influence on *Dove*.

Polytomous Logits have widespread application in banking and insurance sector to model consumer attrition, profitability and risk. Retailing and telecom are the other sectors where applications of such models have been widely reported.

Other 'Separation' Models

Multiple discriminant analysis is an alternative technique when the predictive variable is a nominal or a classification variable. For example, if one were to identify the type of individuals who buy mutual funds, as against ones who do not consider mutual funds as an investment option, based on household/demographic characteristics and other relevant behavioural traits of the respondent, multiple discriminant analysis would be a good approach to develop a classification routine that decides group identities. Note that logit model is also used for classification purposes in such cross-sectional analysis. The only alleged advantage for discriminant analysis, with its ability to estimate multiple discriminant functions (number of functions being related to the number of categories) is its potential to do a far better job at classification than a simple utility formulation used in most MNL models.

However, it is important to note that the construction of the discriminant function is significantly different from the logit model and makes different assumptions regarding the nature of the dependent variable. Logits, on the other hand, are very powerful tools to develop prediction models, given the elasticity determination, while discriminant analysis often times yield good classification models.

We hope this brief description of logit models would have helped the reader appreciate the key model difference in comparison with regression models. While the objectives are similar, regression and logits differ significantly in the approach to construction of the model.

APPENDIX 5

INTERVIEW GUIDE FOR OUR INDUSTRY RESEARCH

The basis for having a discussion with Analytics practitioners is given below. These are broad guidelines that were used to initiate the conversation and thereon flexibility was maintained to ensure that newer issues that emerged during the course of the conversation were explored further.

1. Broad categories of expectations from the 'Analytics' function in your organization.
2. What is accomplished, what is desirable in terms of output, what should be the areas to improve in the next 5 years?
3. What are the immediate constraints in improving productivity of the Analytics function and, the causes of the same—why are they hard to remove?
4. In the long run, what should the industry do to overcome these constraints?
5. Describe the specialist resource available/required in this function—where is it sourced from, their experience profile, skill mix and their future progression—any possible constraints?
6. Describe the leadership role for this function—profile, capabilities, long-term orientation, possible gaps in future leadership.
7. What causes or defeats a thriving Analytics function/ practice in an organization – roles and responsibilities of Analytics functionaries?

8. Why Analytics is important today and why it was not so earlier?

9. What to avoid, unreasonableness in expectations?

APPENDIX 6

SELECT CASES OF ANALYTICS ADOPTION IN INDIAN ORGANIZATIONS

We followed up our business executive study (described in the last chapter) with a more detailed study of five organizations (that we were allowed to visit). The purpose was to investigate in some detail, how data is currently used and processed for business monitoring and decision making. Additionally, we wanted to have a better understanding of the influencers of adoption of knowledge processes (Analytics). Our focus was on India-based (indigenous) organizations.

An Upcoming Hospitality Chain

FOCUS ON MANAGING BUSINESS DATA FOR ENHANCING
THE QUALITY OF INSIGHTS

The hospitality chain maintains two prominent databases of its customers that are used for decision support: (a) transaction (bookings) data for revenue management, accounting and operational monitoring and (b) loyalty database that is used for tracking repeat customers for generating marketing, promotions and customer retention initiatives.

Both these initiatives are managed separately and there is no data integration across these two platforms to manage the information holistically.

Ideally, it may require someone to utilize their planning processes to connect the disparate pieces of information and build a roadmap to leverage the information source for greater organizational use. However, this organization does not have personnel to spare who have enough time to conceptualize such a solution. Most executives are preoccupied with their near-term operational responsibilities to apply their mind on longer-term value additions. The feeling is that 'we shall cross the hurdle when we encounter it'. It was obvious to us that there is no felt need for such initiative and if required, a technology consultant would be hired at a later date to build the infrastructure.

An Oil Refinery

BUILDING A MORE EFFECTIVE MONITORING SYSTEM
FOR THE DECISION MAKER: THROUGHPUT DASH BOARD

While this case does not pertain to the domain of Marketing Analytics, it does provide interesting insights beyond operations (which is the focus in this case).

This refinery (like many) has invested in the distributed control system (DCS) to monitor crude oil refining process operations. This system monitors, displays and stores various stage-wise process parameters along with the plant throughput. A template of the monitoring of the throughput is given below (Figure A6.1). This kind of a monitoring report can be created at appropriate periodicity based on the suitable requirement of the decision makers.

However, the DCS also stores various process parameters (pressure, temperature, etc.) on a continuous basis. In most cases, the data is used in real time to monitor the refining process. However, what is important is that the process data are stored as a time series which can be used to create appropriate aggregate diagnostics. Associations between changes in process parameters (on a periodic basis) can be correlated with variance in output on equivalent time intervals to develop plausible associations (may be causality). Of course, our survey rarely came across such diagnostics. Instead, most process data from the DCS are used by operations managers to monitor plant productivity (Figure A6.2). For productivity review sessions, the data are not looked into formally, but we understand that the personnel responsible for managing operations provide a view based on their experience to senior management. A plausible reason for this 'reluctance' to create a diagnostic report which associates variance in throughput with variance in refining process parameters could be that such reports are not demanded by 'higher authority'. Asymmetry in information availability (and knowledge of information processes) may also create differential power equations within organizations, which many would not like to disrupt without a necessary demand for the same.

Our study also revealed that the idea of attribution modelling (causality) using the DCS data would be of immense help to many plant/operations heads. However, as stated earlier, there are signs of reluctance to change age old procedures and 'ruffle feathers' in the process.

A Process Industry Manufacturing Industrial Chemicals

OPERATIONAL MONITORING VERSUS FUTURISTIC PLANNING

A similar situation prevails at another process plant that was surveyed. This plant produces industrial chemicals. A DCS is available to monitor and record process parameters continuously. Daily and fortnightly throughput and variance from plan is reported to senior management similar to the one described in the earlier case. However, if a variance report has to be discussed for causation, it still has to be at a review

Figure A6.1   Representative Dashboard for Throughput Monitoring: For Senior Management

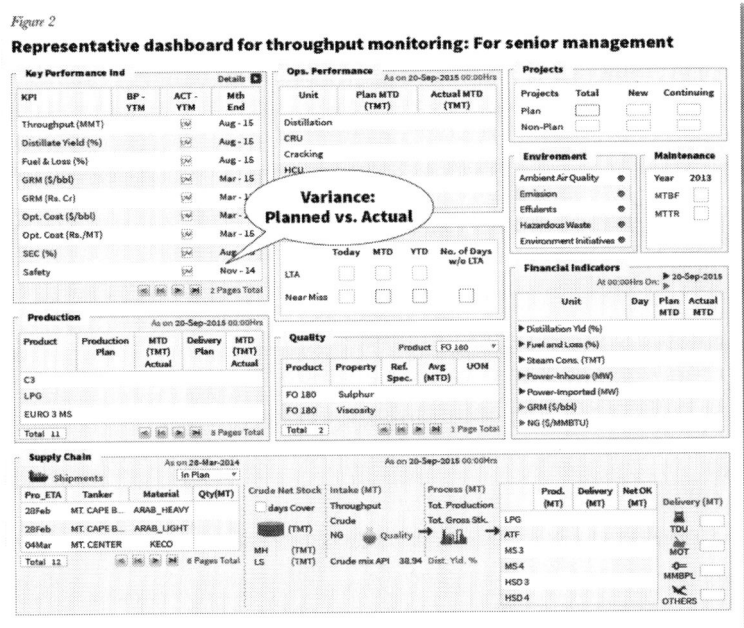

Figure A6.2   Real Time Monitoring of Plant/Process Parameters: Dashboard

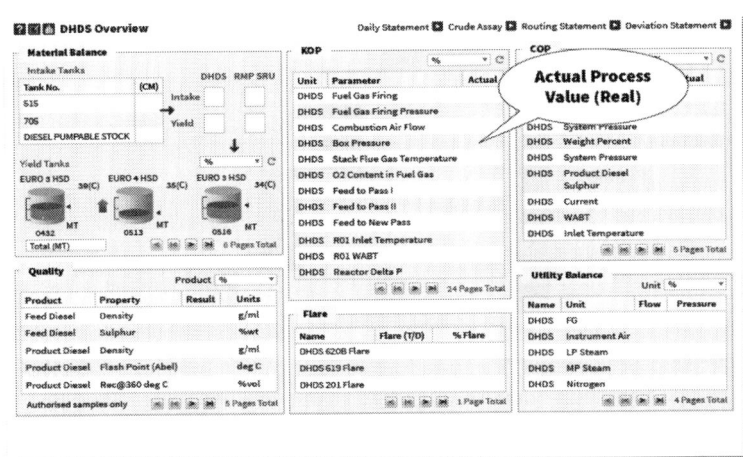

meeting with operations personnel providing a perspective rather than an automated process generating a report on variance in process parameters (causal factors) from the DCS.

Why then is an investment in process control and monitoring system not used optimally? The response is that 'the time is not ripe to question age-old practices'. Why rock the boat when no one is questioning current practices?

It must be pointed out that we also found evidence of employees getting trained in quality management issues and some are skilled to develop reports associating process variance with throughput variances for leakage monitoring in the system. Most of these attempts are however, still sporadic and the information system is not yet being utilized to build a culture to demand higher level diagnostics (Figure A6.3).

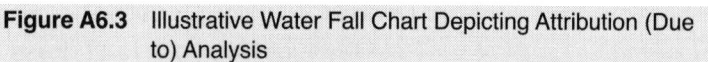

Figure A6.3   Illustrative Water Fall Chart Depicting Attribution (Due to) Analysis

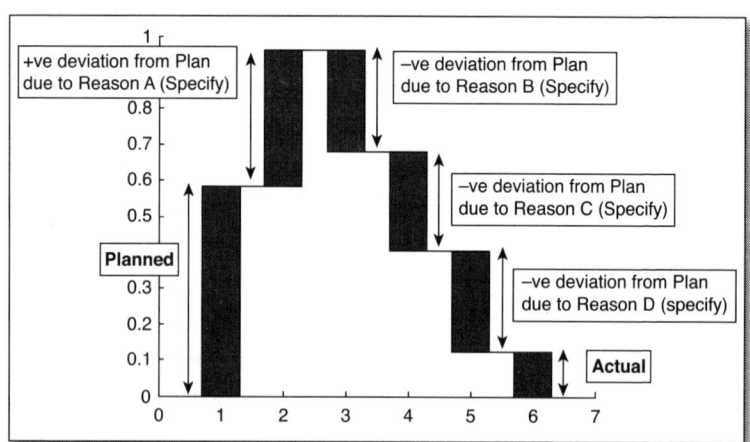

Actual = Planned + (due to Reason A) − (due to Reason B) − (due to Reason C) − (due to Reason D)

A Regional Dairy Products Marketing Organization

A full-portfolio regional dairy product company has product variants that run up to more than a hundred stock keeping units, including milk, processed milk products and tertiary items like chocolates. Milk being a perishable item requires immaculate planning to ensure that wastage is minimized. Such precise planning would actually require a very sophisticated forecasting/planning model.

However, much to our surprise, such concerns about the need for precise forecasting was not found to be of material significance by the management. Historical basis of planning was past consumption behaviour. Our hunch (though not confirmed by the management) is that in spite of a large operation, given that the per capita consumption of milk in India is still very low, production never exceeds the intrinsic consumption capacity. Hence, planning rarely leads to over production since supply is almost always lower than market demand. Additionally, the production cycle being daily, production planning can be recalibrated at a very high frequency to address stock piling issues, especially for highly perishable items.

Hence, from a market planning perspective, this dairy organization still relies on experience and hunches and collective wisdom of its dairy union members and it has worked fine for them so far. Analytics may not have a very important role in such environments for now.

A Stock Trading Platform

Useful information regarding stock brokers and the type of transaction that they effect is recorded daily that provides insights about broker activity and quantity/quality/nature of transaction. Currently, most of the analysis of this data is about monitoring trade and attrition (loss of volume, if any).

Proactive analysis for providing consultative services to brokers on transaction quality and optimal business is not part of the deliverables for the trading platform managers.

Again, performance monitoring of the trading activity with the generated data is not considered to be a primary activity. Many potentially interesting and creative ideas were discussed about optimal utilization of data, but were summarily dismissed from an implementation point of view due to 'legal constraints'.

So What Did We Conclude?

The organizations studied are seen to have significant (though not comprehensive) information resources to plan their analytical processes in alignment with their business decision support. This contradicts, to some extent, the perception created based on the business executive survey. It is noted that the adoption of analytic practices across industries is varied in spite of similar resource availability and potential. We feel, based on our discussions, this is largely attributable to the lack of exogenous imperatives that spur such activities. The perceived need is still largely dormant.

Be that as it may, it may just take one foresighted organization to break the 'inertia' barrier for such a practice to become an industry standard.

Implications of the Findings

There is seemingly a lack of motivation (rightly or otherwise) among many organization leaders to look beyond the normal operational usage of business database. Numerous attempts to enquire regarding how improvements can be brought into the analytical prowess have been met with guarded optimism and often times seemingly little enthusiasm. The lack of 'self-criticism' that is observed in many domestic organizations is naturally bewildering and goes against the popular sentiments expressed in trade publications on the potential of Analytics in business organizations.

We propose a few postulates based on this rather subdued perception of analytics adoption in Indian businesses. Our strong prior is that:

1. It has not caught the senior management's imagination and hence it is still low priority in many organizations. Nowhere did we find the senior executives very involved in discussions regarding their internal capabilities in analytics. This could be a reason for the lack of an appetite (culture) for analytics.

2. Decision makers find it difficult to discern the value of analytics. Hence, their ability to provide direction in developing this capability is limited.

3. Some organizations may expect turnkey solutions to their problems and do not have internal resources to spare for development initiatives. They depend upon vendors who largely sell 'product solutions' rather than 'solutions to problems' and hence the issues remain unaddressed fully.

4. No one in the industry has taken significant steps to improve Analytical capabilities in their respective organization and hence it is not a priority (on competitive benchmark).

5. There is confusion over what is the true scope of Analytics. Is it a tool box or process to generate insights from data for supporting decision making? There are more than one explanation for what Analytics stands for and hence little clarity on what needs to be done.

6. It reduces information control among a few savvy employees and therefore disrupts traditional operating style of

the management. Hence, it is not favoured by some employees unless there is an imposition from the top.

7. There is a significant disconnect between Analytics competent employees (centred around the IS function) and the business decision makers. Hence, there is no common talking platform to develop new and useful data-driven decision support applications.

It appears that asymmetric information control, inadequate 'felt' need, top management's unfamiliarity with the potential, near-term exigent requirements and unrealistic expectations from turnkey solutions seem to be some of the reasons impeding the adoption of an appropriate analytics culture in some of these organizations.

This trend may continue for a while, and as mentioned earlier, until the market parameters in India change radically for business organizations to feel the 'heat' of Analytics. This fact is corroborated by Germann et al. (2012) who find that level of competition is positively correlated with the depth of Marketing Analytics used in firms.

Final Comments

We made an attempt to evaluate the Analytics process adoption in organizations across industries in India. The findings are largely based on discussions and interviews with key management personnel and their direct reports. We have identified some areas in which there is potential to develop impactful analytics.

Unlike the business executive survey, our in-depth case studies revealed that organizations (at least some) have a large repository of data which are primarily used for operational purposes. The transitioning towards strategic applications is yet to take off in many places for reasons provided in an earlier section.

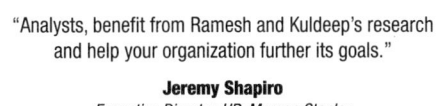

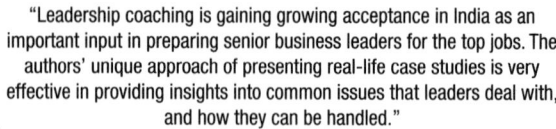

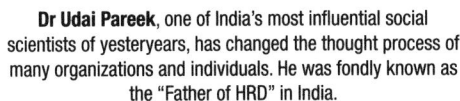
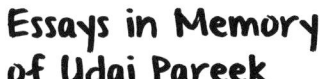